# *Now* you tell me!

# 12 ACTORS GIVE THE BEST ADVICE THEY NEVER GOT

**FEATURING**

CHARLES BUSCH · JOSEPH KOLINSKI · MICHAEL MCKEAN
BRIAN STOKES MITCHELL · JULIA MOTYKA · ALEXANDRA NEIL
MICHAEL O'NEIL · DAVE OYELOWO · PAULEY PERRETTE
EDEN SHER · BRENDA STRONG
SAM WATERSON

AND THE **LAST MAJOR INTERVIEW** BY LYNN REDGRAVE

# SHERIDAN SCOTT · CHRIS WILLMAN

## TODD COLEMAN

Arundel Publishing
P.O. Box 377
Warwick, NY 10990
www.arundelpublishing.com
www.nowyoutellmebooks.com

ISBN 978-1-933608-25-9
First Edition April 2012
Printed in the United States of America.

# TABLE OF CONTENTS

# LYNN REDGRAVE

## "Make Things Happen"

Lynn Redgrave's extraordinary career spanned five decades and four continents. She starred on London's West End and on Broadway, in film and television, and worked for directors from Laurence Olivier, Franco Zeffirelli, and Noël Coward to James Ivory and Bill Condon. Ms. Redgrave had two Oscar nominations, thirty years apart, for her roles in the films *Georgy Girl* and *Gods and Monsters*. She won two Golden Globes, an Independent Spirit Award, and a New York Film Critics Circle Award, and was nominated for two Screen Actors Guild Awards as well as an Emmy for her situation comedy, *House Calls*. A member of the distinguished Redgrave clan of actors, she was also a successful playwright.

# MAKING A LIVING

## AUDITIONS

Some people recommend showing up looking as near to the role as possible—if you're going for the housekeeper, don't turn up in your Chanel suit—and that is probably good advice. Although I remember my father [Sir Michael Redgrave] telling me back in the old days that he was sitting in on some auditions being held at the Old Vic, where he was already a member of the company. Suddenly, they heard a terrible clanking noise from offstage. This young woman had hired real armor and clanked on to audition and could barely move! He used that as an example of taking it a step too far.

When I was still in drama school, I heard about an audition for *A Midsummer Night's Dream* directed by Tony Richardson. I decided to go to the audition, thinking, "Why not? Either I'll get the part—though not likely—or I'll get valuable practice." And I ended up being offered the role of Helena. Taking it would mean I would have to leave drama school a semester early—to the absolute horror of the principal of the school. He told me, "You can't possibly do this!" and he proceeded to name a couple of people at the drama school who if *they* were the ones [to leave early], then that would be fine—but not me. That made me so cross, I took the part at once.

I did an audition for my second film, *Girl with Green Eyes*, which I did before *Georgy Girl*. The film was based on a novel by Edna O'Brien, an Irish writer. When I got to the theater, it was wall-to-wall Aran sweaters and Irish accents—what chance did I have? I became incredibly nervous. When it was my turn, I got up; and even as I was auditioning, I thought, "This is absolutely dreadful!" Then, lo and behold, I got a callback. So my thinking turned around: "I must have been quite good!" I went back, this time with a lot of confidence, and did my audition again for the director of the theater and the producer. After I auditioned they said, "We called you back because we've seen you onstage at the National Theatre and you were wonderful—but when you did your audition, you were so bad that we thought we had to give you another chance!" Now, the odds of that happening—getting called back because you were so bad—are, in reality, nonexistent! To me, this always illustrated the importance of having confidence when you audition.

I've heard directors say that during auditions they can tell if someone is a possibility within the first couple of minutes. When I sat in on auditions for a play I'd written called *The Mandrake Root*, I found that to be true. I knew right away if a person made me sit up and look, if he or she demanded your attention. I'm inclined to think that one should make a bold step at what one thinks the character should be—but I've heard people say no, because the director might be looking for another sort of performance. I still say, go for it.

To tell you the truth, I am incredibly relieved that I don't need to audition anymore before being offered a part. I'm shocked at some of my colleagues who are made to audition even when they have an amazing body of work that the people must have seen. And I admire today's actors who look on every audition as an opportunity to act.

## KEEPING IT FRESH

The best advice I got about keeping your stage performance fresh was from my father. He did many long runs and short runs; and every performance, he'd choose a point in the play when he had to make an entrance, and he'd invent a different set of circumstances that led him to the door. The circumstances would be in keeping with the play, and he'd do the scene the way it was meant to be, but just by changing one incident, it shakes up your thinking and gives you a new way into the material. For example, you can decide that you came by public transport and now you're late. Or it was raining outside. Or you had a difficult phone call before arriving. Nothing that will change it completely for your fellow actors but something that changes it just enough to make it fresh for you.

The truth is, every performance is different because the audience is a different animal every single night. The play can never be the same because the makeup of the audiences, and the energy coming from the audience, is never the same. Will they laugh at the same time? Will they react the same way to the serious parts?

If you're doing a well-written role in a substantial play, you should never think you are "done," no matter the length of the run.

A lot of actors do feel that. Perhaps one culprit is working somewhere like Williamstown Theatre, or weekly rep in England. They do some great stuff, but they cram that rehearsal period. You're lucky if it's three weeks and you're doing Chekhov. Then you're done after four or five weeks. The show's over, and you go on to the next. The problem with the shortcut is that people could get into the habit of taking on very short runs, which takes away the whole development process. Then suddenly, you come to a show that has three, six, or even nine months of a run, but you're used to three or four weeks and you're done. So now the actors are counting the days because they're bored. When you come to that point—or the point where you think you're "done" developing a role—that's the point at which you rethink!

I came to a very difficult juncture when I was doing *St. Joan* for Circle in the Square for rather the opposite reason. I had done the part before at the Goodman in Chicago. After two sets of rehearsals and countless performances, I reached a point in the pivotal trial scene when I was played out and thought I didn't know where to go. I was stuck, and it felt terrible. There was one performance when I felt I wasn't there. It was awful—but it caused me to remember that there is never an end to exploration. The trial scene is terrifying; and if I was stuck there, I had to back up and rethink how I approached the scenes leading up to it; in fact, I rethought how I was preparing for the whole role.

## LOSING YOUR NERVE

Worst of all for an actor is losing your nerve. It happened to me back in 1975 when I toured with some one-act plays by Michael Frayn called *The*

*Two of Us*. We had done really well on the tour, had gotten good reviews, and had good audiences. Then we got invited to go out to Los Angeles for a brief run.

It was at the Hartington Theater, now called the Doolittle. Opening night, I was backstage—and there was this feeling. It can happen anywhere, certainly in L.A.—but it was this palpable, edgy feeling from the audience of "Okay, show us" just before the curtain went up. It scared the wits out of me. We didn't get good reviews, and consequently we got small audiences; and I really lost my nerve. That's the only time I really and truly lost my nerve. Only actors for whom that has happened can know what I'm talking about. You have gone to the most horrible place you can ever go; you might never get over it. It has certainly kept a lot of people off the stage.

Finishing the run of that play was excruciating. I had this hole in the pit of my stomach, and it was absolutely terrifying, because I had never had that feeling before. I'd never been paralyzed onstage. It got to the point when I thought, "I'm going to have to give up the theater. I love theater, I love film acting as well, but I can't do it. This is terrible." Afterward, I was in a depression.

And then I got this offer to do a play at Lincoln Center in New York that was just gorgeous. I thought, "I have to do that—I just have to." Fortunately for me, [AcademyAward-winning and Emmy-winning] actress Ruth Gordon was also in the cast. It was Ruth Gordon who showed me how to get my nerve back. The way she approached the role, the way she prepared was so inspirational and so disciplined and so brilliant that you just knew that her performance was no longer corruptible by a difficult night or a difficult audience. During that show, I learned a lot from her. I probably learned more than I did during my years at drama school. I got back my nerve. And if you can find yourself back in a place where it's the most natural thing in the world to be onstage, once you've come back from that horrible place, you will never go there again.

## SECRETS OF THE INCORRUPTIBLE PERFORMANCE

Ruth's secret of building an incorruptible performance was all in the preparation.

First of all, it was the way she used rehearsals. She arrived on the first day with her lines already memorized.

Earlier, when I'd worked with Noël Coward in his production of *Hay Fever*, he insisted that we all learn the lines beforehand. We all thought we were the fabulous young things of this generation and, oh, how old-fashioned of him. But, in fact, we arrived with the lines learned. And he was right. We used the four weeks of rehearsal interacting with one another and exploring the parts instead of with our heads in the book. We were able to look our fellow actors in the eye from day one. It was fantastic. Olivier prelearned *Othello;* he said you can't play a role such as Othello if your five weeks of rehearsal are taken up with learning your lines. You've lost your time for exploration.

Ruth was like that. So, eager to be up there with her, I learned my lines right away.

But it was more than that. For example, if there was business in a scene in which she'd have to pour a cup of tea and get the tea over to the table and give a line, she practiced all that at home so that when she came in, it was just a matter of making it smooth and with the other actors. Ruth said rehearsal is not for going over and over those little bits. It's up to me to get those smooth so that I can work with the other actors. She would rehearse herself at home in the shoes she was going to be wearing in the play and in a rehearsal skirt so there wasn't one moment when those things held her up. Consequently, every day she was free to rehearse with the other actors and explore the role.

## LEARNING LINES

There are many actors who say, "I can't really learn my lines till I know where I'm moving." Honestly, that's a cop out. An opera singer doesn't say, "I can't sing my aria until I know where I'm walking." It's just not done. The ideal to me is, learn your lines so you're free to play them any which way, not learn them because at this moment when I say my outburst, I know I'm going to be throwing myself onto the sofa and I'm going to be really sobbing and I'm going to be saying it really loudly. You work with so many directors who change it every time. If you can only remember that you say, "Oh, good morning. How are you?" when you move left, what are you going to do when he says, "Don't move?"

Once you're in the scene with the other person, your take on the scene is probably going to change; but if you know your lines and they're inside you, you can call on them in the most brilliant way. It's hard, and it takes a lot of discipline. Especially now, for me, it takes two or three times as long to memorize my lines as it used to because I'm older. Even though I work a lot and do get a lot of practice, it still takes longer.

If you prelearn your lines, you also have to sometimes put up with the slight displeasure of those who don't believe in this because they're shown up a bit. It's kind of spoiling it for them that everybody isn't going at their same pace. Stay polite. Stay respectful. Everybody has his or her own way—but that doesn't mean you have to follow it!

As you rehearse, you'll often work with someone who is having difficulty or who is quite frankly not putting in the hard work that you are. You can't do anything about that. You have to go on and do whatever is going to help you grow the most.

## MOVING BETWEEN FILM, TELEVISION, AND STAGE

The first difference, I think, between acting in the theater, rather than on television or on film, is that in a movie, the actors have no control. Not in how the shot is framed, not in when the camera will be on you or whether it will be a close-up, not in the editing, not even in whether your best scene will be cut from the film altogether. Not in whether the film is heavily promoted and becomes a hit or whether it goes straight to DVD. It's something you have to understand going in. You do your part to the very best of your ability, but it is a director's medium.

The opposite is also true: a lot of what an audience detects about what is going on with your character has to do with the editing. No actor has ever won an Oscar without brilliant editing.

**In acting, there is nothing as powerful as complete stillness.**

On the stage, if you want to convey extreme distress, it often has to be accompanied by some physical movement. It cannot be read in the back row unless your shoulders go back or your whole body tenses up. But on camera, if it's a close-up, if you truly think the thought, something happens. A thought and a feeling, the slightest change in skin color because of the emotion underneath the line or the moment, can be detected by a camera. It's remarkable. Liz Norman said that she never wore any makeup when working on film because then the camera can see your skin change color and the audience can see it.

I will say that both onstage and on film, there is nothing as powerful as complete stillness. It may be the very lack of movement that gets the audience's attention.

## OUT OF ORDER

There is a big difference in how you develop a character on film as opposed to onstage. Onstage you have a gestation period: reading, going through all the stages of dress rehearsal, technical rehearsal, and finally performing for the audience. On film, invariably, the scenes are all shot out of order. I had an interesting discussion with David Green, the director who did the remake of *What Ever Happened to Baby Jane?* with me and my sister [Vanessa Redgrave]. I was talking about continuity, and the fact that you might have to do the final important scene on your first day of shooting. David said he once had the opportunity to do a film in sequence. It was a TV film, and he said he would never do that again. I said, "Why? It must have been quite fascinating for the actors." He said that during the first couple of days, the leading actor really hadn't nailed his character. As they went on, his character developed. However, as the audience watched the film, the impression they got was from the first bit, and that first impression wasn't very good. David now feels that when you film out of sequence, perhaps at first your character isn't as strong as it will be after you've been playing it a while; but those first scenes are kind of buried with the whole film, and the audience has already made an opinion of the character, so you can get away with it. Often, if the audience has been enjoying a film from the start, they will even read into a scene something that was never actually there. David said he would never again want to do something in sequence.

I find film acting a bit like cooking. Say you are making a stew. You have a taste, and it needs a bit more salt; then it needs thickening up a bit; and, oh, it needs more bay leaf. When you are doing a role in a film, it's a bit like that. You do your first two days, and maybe you feel you have been too jolly. Maybe

> **Film acting is like cooking a stew or a complicated Christmas cake.**

you've talked to the director, or you've realized it on your own; but that's okay, because now you say, "I've done enough of that; now I'll add a bit more salt or vinegar." It's like a stew or a complicated Christmas cake. Bit by bit you're discovering layers of character and building the performance. Some of them are internal. Often, for film, external choices and discoveries are every bit as important. A particular example of that for me was the movie *Gods and Monsters*.

## HANNA, NOT LYNN

Developing the character of Hanna, and the look for her character, I worked very closely with the director, Bill Condon, who is just a genius. I knew I shouldn't wear a lot of makeup—although she should have a red lipstick because she would try really hard. I was working against the fact that I can very easily look aristocratic in that kind of English way, and Hanna was Hungarian and not aristocratic at all. In the script it said her hair was pulled up tight with a bun on top as if she is in the Frankenstein movie; but I knew that would make me look like an aristocrat. So I said, "Let me work out something I can do with my own hair," because I knew that if I was to be believed as Hanna, I couldn't wear a wig. Often people know when there is a prosthesis or a wig. They know when it's a trick, and there can't be any of that.

On the first day, we were doing the scene when Hanna is waving good-bye to Brendan Fraser's character, who is going off to a party. The next day Bill said to me, "There is this moment when you are watching them go off; and I don't know what it is, but I see Lynn, and I'm not seeing Hanna."

I said, "Let me look at it." He showed me, and I could see it. It was a physical thing: as Hanna I could never hold my chin up in the air. It was a small moment and very technical, but when I lifted my chin and smiled, I looked like Lynn. It was okay in the wider shots. I asked if he could do without my close-up there, and Bill said, "Oh, absolutely."

Bill was so smart to tell me, because he knew I would be able to fix it. In fact, in *Gods and Monsters* I felt that I got the closest to what my drama school aspiration was, which was to be so much the character that you're not instantly recognized. In many cases that happened. People didn't notice it was me until the credits rolled because I did manage to get rid of Lynn and my mannerisms (like everybody, I have many) and tried to just be Hanna.

I give a lot of the credit to Bill Condon because he's got the most brilliant way with actors. He has a wonderful way of helping and editing and shaping; but he totally respects actors, and if he casts somebody, then a lot of the job is up to them to present the character.

My physical appearance was also important to the character I played for Bill in *Kinsey*. My character's scene is only three minutes long, at the end of the film; but her impact on Kinsey is profound. So Bill Condon came round to my apartment, and we talked about what the character's look should be. That was really important, because you were only going to see her for such a brief moment of time. I said, "I think she becomes this angel of light at Kinsey's moment of deepest depression. Kinsey feels all he's done is wasted.

She's the one who makes him think that it isn't. If you like the idea, I think I should be in light-colored clothes and that I should have white hair."

At the time I had no hair because I was still going through chemo for breast cancer, so we could do anything we wanted. We went off to the wig makers together with Bruce [Finlayson, the costume designer], and I tried on lots of wigs. I said, "I have a feeling that this character is one of those soccer mums who always had one of those wash-and-wear-haircuts and just never changed it." We ended up with pale hair, and the kind of clothes that were fashionable when she was young. It's not every director who has such an eye and knows what he want when he sees it. But Bill loves working with actors; he loves the process and wants to understand it and be a part of it. He's just brilliant.

## DIFFICULT DIRECTORS

Working with a difficult director comes back to that total basic understanding and acceptance that you have no control over the situation. What is particularly difficult for young actors is when they're coming in for one or two day's work and they can't go out too much on a limb because this is the only opportunity they have to play this character. If directors don't like what they see, they might not have the vision or the knowledge of your other work to know that you can change it. So no matter how difficult the director is being, be respectful and know that he or she is the one running the army.

It's also amazing how many directors are devoid of good ideas for blocking, or what an actor might be doing in a scene. Consequently, it's always a good idea to have given it some thought yourself. Always present your ideas positively, such as, "How would you feel if I was to be at the kitchen table chopping the potatoes?" or whatever. If you're asked to do something that isn't working and you know it feels so terrible, rather than go, "I feel terrible doing this!" come up with something positive. "Oh, I've just come up with this; what do you think?" If you get shot down, then you just have to grin and bear it and decide you're going to be real and connected even though it isn't making a lot of sense to you at all.

## YOUR BEST FRIENDS ON THE MOVIE SET

When you arrive on set for your first few films, there are things that will likely be confusing, and no one is going to explain them to you; members of the cast and crew all have their own job and assume you know what you're doing. Even if something goes wrong, don't jump to the conclusion that it's going to be a horrible day. It can be a wonderful day if you stay calm.

It's very helpful, on every movie set, to have a good rapport with the camera people. When you arrive on set, simply go up and introduce yourself. They can tell you many things you need to know. First of all, I always find out how close-in the shot is and where the frame of the camera cuts off. You can't always tell from where the lens is, and it's very important to know or suddenly the director will be freaking out because you're out of frame.

Then make friends with prop people because they are your absolute best friends. They are your absolute best friends because, if you have an idea about cutting potatoes or making an omelet, they love collaborating. If I was to ask the director and if he liked the idea of my character cutting potatoes, it comes down to the prop people as to whether potatoes can be gotten.

In *Gods and Monsters* there's a scene in which Brendan Fraser's character asks Hanna about whether she's married. The script only said, "Hanna's in the kitchen." I said to the prop guy, "Could I have any eggs; how hard would that be?" He said, "Not hard at all. There's a market down the road." So after finding out I could get eggs, I went to Bill Condon and said, "How would it be if I made an omelet? I can really beat the eggs and do some business with the eggs." He said, "Oh, I like that."

So the prop people went off to buy dozens of eggs. After that it became fun to collaborate with them. They started coming to me and asking, "What tray do you think Hanna would like? We've got this and this, but for tomorrow I was thinking I've got this sister who has a silver tray . . ." So we started really getting into it.

I think the more you say "hello" and introduce yourself to the crew, the more you don't feel that you are out on a limb.

Also, make sure you introduce yourself to the assistant director. The A.D. is running the set. He's the one who is the boss of the set and making it all work for the director. If you know his or her name and you have introduced yourself, then you are already on a better footing. Even if it's your first film and you're not well-known yet, the A.D. will probably start calling you by your name. It's all just making a place of comfort for yourself, because then you can do good work.

## YOU LOOK GORGEOUS

Surprisingly, in this business, having great physical beauty can be quite difficult. On the one hand, fantastically beautiful people may feel that they aren't taken quite as seriously, and they're probably right. It's human nature. On the other hand, beauty can give you instant rewards: "My God, that person is so attractive! Quick, put them in the show!" If great beauty combines with talent, it's stunning.

**Plastic surgery can be the biggest shortcut to oblivion.**

The hardest thing about physical beauty is that we all age, and then what?

I never was a great physical beauty, so I don't have the insecurity of trying to keep my looks. But I do remember, in the sixties, ironing my hair on the ironing board because I had to have this incredible sleek look, going on endless diets, wearing the right makeup, and all those things.

The hardest thing, I think, is to grow into your own looks in a sort of dignified way so you're not desperately trying to remain a young version of yourself. Especially out West, women in show business turn to an enormous amount of plastic surgery. In the end, if you are sixty and you try to make yourself look thirty, they are not going to cast you as a thirty-year-old. What nobody tells them, and I'll tell them right now, is that plastic surgery can be the biggest shortcut to oblivion, especially in response to the natural signs of aging. While it is true that the business is very ageist, if you can get past the middle part, there comes a whole other thing where you can play that old

Russian grandmother, or other parts that can be fascinating. But if you've had a lot of surgery, you're going to miss out on all those roles. What do you do in the business of expression with a face from which expression has been removed? There are one or two people who have had the surgery done brilliantly, but only one or two. Most of us can spot it a mile off. It scares the wits out of me when I see people get scared and feel they can't age. Or if they've begun on that route and feel, "Oh my God, I have to have it again; I can beat it!" Whether it's Botox or you name it, you just have to keep grounded.

## NEW YORK OR L.A.?

If you're starting out, trying to decide between New York or L.A., I would say New York. True, there's more lucrative work in L.A. because there are a lot of shows shot there. New York has some, but not as many. But the theater is not respected on the West Coast. I'm not saying there aren't good theaters; there are. But it's not respected in the same way.

I do think that the theater is the only place where you can truly stretch. If you're lucky enough to go from guest shot to guest shot on a bunch of shows in L.A., you're working maybe two days at a time. You can't take big risks because you may be just outside of what they imagined for that role. You have to be middle-of-the-roadish and just fit in. So you're not stretching yourself. If you are wanting to get experience and wanting to play a host of things, go to one of the theater festivals such as Ashland or anyplace like that.

In order to do regional theater, you're probably going to audition in New York. Most regional theaters have a New York casting director.

## DRY SPELLS

Dry spells are rough for actors. Even if his paintings aren't selling, a painter can still go paint. My younger daughter is a photographer; and even when she is just struggling to pay the rent, she can go shoot photos and come up with something. But actors can't really act unless we're employed. You can go to class, and that's a good thing; but there is nothing like working for a paycheck that concentrates the mind!

What kept me sane during the first really bad dry spell that came along was deciding I had to make myself a job. But what to do? I was always making excuses. I thought if I was a writer, I would write myself a great part such as Shirley Valentine. But of course I'm not a writer; why would I think I'm a writer?

But I had time, and I started working with material that was very accessible to me: my relationship with my father. The material became a one-woman play: *Shakespeare for My Father*.

Once I started writing my own material, it changed the way I looked at everything. I can always feel as if I am a busy, creative person because I am, even if someone isn't offering me a job; I make things happen. I'm a great believer that if you put out energy, something is attracted to it. I don't know why or how that is.

## WHEN YOU'VE BEEN DONE DIRT

What do you do when you feel you've been done dirt by someone? Oh boy—that's a tough one. It does happen. I have certainly come across it myself. It's terribly hard to hang in there, and yet anger is very destructive. It can be a very brutal business. Recently, I read about a plum role that was basically cast; but another actor went full on—"You have to have me; you have to have me"—and was apparently good enough to get the role. But that was undoubtedly little comfort to the other actor who was dumped at the last second. You have to somehow let it go because it can eat you up; but I don't know any real

---

### RUTH GORDON'S SECRETS OF THE INCORRUPTIBLE PERFORMANCE

#### Before rehearsals

- Memorize your lines.
- Practice the bits of business (like pouring tea) while delivering your lines until the action is smooth.
- Wear the shoes, skirt, or anything else you will wear during the performance while practicing at home.

#### This allows you to

- Use rehearsal time to interact with the other actors and explore your part.
- Play with and truly explore your lines.
- Be flexible as the director gives you instructions.

It's all in the preparation.

For more go to http://www .nowyoutellmebooks.com/actors

advice on how you let go, how you stop thinking, "That could have been me." You have to then strike out and say, "There's going to be something else."

I have a friend who was offered a great role on Broadway; but she was already in something off-Broadway, and the producer simply wouldn't release her. The woman they cast instead went on to huge success: in fact, she won a Tony and went on to be in the movie. There's a bit inside you that keeps going, "That could have been me!" But I think you just have to say, "It might not have been. Just the fact someone else won a Tony doesn't mean I was going to. It might not have been my lucky day. Maybe what happened was exactly right." You just have to let go and put your best foot forward.

## WHEN IS IT TIME TO GIVE UP ACTING AND DO SOMETHING ELSE?

I do have a simple answer for that. If there's something else you can actually picture yourself doing, you should do it. Sometimes a bit of a reality check is not a bad idea.

Those who consider acting as a career need three essential things. The first is talent, but there are millions of people with talent. It's in our schools, in our colleges, in the community theater down the road. The second is the absolute need to act: a consuming passion. It has to be so strong that you think you could not live without it. The third is the resilience to get past the day with the horrible director who treats you like a piece of dirt because you are only playing a small role, the resilience to continually put yourself out there and go for those auditions and find a way to always do your best work. The need and the resilience can't be taught, but I think it does separate those who can make it from those who can't.

My middle child (I say child, but all my children are grown, and I have grandchildren) trained to be an actress. She was very talented. She had a good start, did some work off-Broadway, did a lot of workshops, had a small recurring role on *All My Children*. She loved the actual acting. But she realized that she just didn't have this ingredient that made her go out there and go after something no matter what.

It might have been easier for her to know it because of our family. She'd seen those of us who have pursued it all our lives, including some of her cousins, have that obsession, that "I *have* to do it; I'm bouncing back from this disappointment, and I'm carrying on." Thank goodness she did realize. She became a teacher. And so many different aspects of all her acting, her directing, her theater training have been put to very good use with the children. It is wonderfully fulfilling for her.

## MOVING ON

I have been on the board of trustees of the Actors Fund for some time. They have a fantastic program to assist people who need to transition out of the profession for whatever reason. It may be because they are dancers and they get injured; but quite often it's because maybe actors have had some success but they've reached a point where they can't make ends meet doing what they love. The Fund has an actors' work program where they can meet with somebody and discuss all the things you could do. They interview you to discover what kinds of natural gifts you have, maybe for something you have never thought of before. Then they help you get trained for it. Some have gone on to really wonderful careers in completely different fields through the Actors Fund. They're also probably continuing to act in community theater, or directing at a school or something. Very high satisfaction.

# MAKING A LIFE

## ACTORS AND MONEY

Acting is a strange profession when it comes to money. Perhaps the most difficult thing is when young actors get sudden success; suddenly loads of TV work that allow them to think, "I'm making so much money—this is fantastic!" It's hard when you're young to realize that work and money don't follow a straight path. Never ever live in a way that relies on a large amount of money continuously coming in. Sometimes when you have become accustomed to living in a certain way, it limits the kinds of jobs you can consider taking. I've heard so many people say, "I can't afford to do a play." That's just horrible! It's true that off-Broadway and not-for-profit theaters are a fall in pay, but it's not just about the money. When you do a wonderful play, it's an investment: if it goes well, people may see it—and you have to make sure people do come to see it! But as far as lifestyle, keep your feet on the ground and keep your overhead not ridiculous.

**Keep your feet on the ground and your overhead not ridiculous.**

People probably think I'm crazy saying this, but young people who get early success fall into thinking they have to have an agent, and a manager and a business manager and a press agent. Before you know it, a huge percentage of your salary is gone keeping your people employed. It's insane! There are definitely times when you need a press agent. I have a press agent right now and have had for a while now, but I've been at it for a very long time. I do have an agent, but I don't have a manager; I've never had a manager. With all due respect to some very good managers, I don't know what all that is about. I can see a situation where you're starring in a TV show—even if it's a hit, it could be canceled any day. But if you're suddenly supporting a "team," you know they will make themselves indispensable.

When your career takes off, you have to keep those feet on the ground, planted in real life. You run a danger when you ricochet into this false realm of fame, and suddenly you feel like you can't be regular folk. Once you can't be regular folk, how are you going to play regular folk? You can only play a theatrical projection of what regular folk do.

I love New York City. I think there is nothing like public transport and being out there with all kinds of people. The wonderful thing about the New York subway is that nobody looks at each other. I look at absolutely everybody! Every day is an acting lesson. You see the body language of these people, how they sit with the people sitting on either side of them, and it's fascinating. I'm storing it all away. I like to try and guess before I've heard in their voices what nationality they are. I can usually tell English people—they have a

**Be wary of the trappings of fame. Once you can't be regular folk, how are you going to play regular folk? You can only play a theatrical projection of what regular folk do.**

whole different body language. Even from across a street I can tell people are English. I get near enough to hear their accent, and, oh yes, they're English.

## THE TENSION BETWEEN FAMILY AND WORK

*In 1981, Ms. Redgrave was nominated for an Emmy for her starring role in the television sitcom* House Calls. *In between seasons, she gave birth to her daughter Annabel. When she requested that it be written into her contract that she could bring her baby to her dressing room on the set, not only was her request denied, but she was ultimately fired from the show. She took the case to court and lost.*

It was an absolutely appalling time in my life. I was a new mom who was breast-feeding her daughter, so I wanted to have her near me. It simply made sense; it's documented over and over again that there is more productivity from a parent who doesn't have to drive forty miles to get their child to day care and leave them there; but if they can go visit them at lunchtime, if they can nurse their children, there's more productivity.

[Losing my job and having many in the industry turn on me] was absolutely horrible, and it was very scary. In a way, it was interesting from an acting point of view to hear people lying under oath.

The only helpful thing is that I can look back now and know my taking a stand did make a difference. At the point when this happened to me, not one studio in L.A.—or anywhere—had day care facilities for children. Forget about the fact that actors ought to have the right to do whatever they want in their dressing rooms, but what about the camera people? Or anyone else on the set?

I lost my suit; and for some years things were very, very difficult. And while I didn't benefit in any way, I guess you could say I lost the battle but won the war. There is not an actress since that has ever been told she cannot bring her child to a dressing room. Things have completely changed. I worked recently with an actress who had her little child with her; because she had the lead in the film, it was in her contract that every two hours she was going to go back and see her baby in her dressing room. Such a thing was unheard of in those days!

I told her the story of me and Annabel, and her jaw was just dropping. I said, "It makes me so happy to see you with your baby because what we went through was worth it." Sometimes you have to stand up for what you believe is right.

## BEING AN ACTOR AND A PARENT

My sister and I have talked over the years about some of the regrets that come with the business. About how you've got a matinee, but that's also the day of your child's school play or concert. You remember the times when you couldn't be there and felt so bad. You wonder about what damage it might or might not do to your child's sense of self and wanting their parents there. On the other hand, many actors' children get a very interesting life. Certainly my kids traveled a lot! I'd take them out of school to places where I was shooting. And, of course, as an actor, you're not working fifty weeks a year with two weeks' holiday. So while they miss out during the run of a play on mummy being there at bedtime, then maybe the three months after that you can do absolutely everything for them, which a parent who had a nine-to-five job couldn't do.

My son, who is my oldest, says that, looking back, there were times he just hated the fact that I wasn't there or that I was going to work at night—but then he looks at all the things he got to do because I was an actor that he never would have done.

It's hard! I think everybody has to make those decisions themselves. A lot of it depends on what sort of backup you can put into place: do you have a parent who can fill in, or good friends; or can you afford help? In the past I saw actresses put off having children because they felt they couldn't juggle it, but it's amazing what you can do when you just rally. You can do it.

## FAMILY LIFE IN THE PUBLIC EYE

Living life in the public eye is a very mixed blessing. On the plus side, as with [my niece] Natasha [Richardson]'s death, we were all completely overwhelmed at the kindness of strangers who perhaps hadn't even met Natasha but felt that they knew her. I mean, we all just had this kind of outpouring of people saying it hit them, too. We can't quite figure that out because we can't step back from ourselves. On the other hand, it can be sort of difficult and intrusive, as when the paparazzi were at the hospital [where she died] trying to get pictures of my great-nephews. That feels really grotesque at such a difficult time.

But my sister, my brother, and I have all had many years of living in the public eye, and we don't really get bothered by people. That's mainly because we go out and about among people; we're not hiding behind closed doors and getting out of dark-shaded limos. We're just not.

I know it must be hellish to be one of the big movie stars who can't move without people writing about them. But on the other hand, you see people who are being so bothered by the paparazzi, yet they go to the places where the paparazzi hang out. They certainly don't *have* to go to that club where only famous people go. But everybody has his or her own idea.

## TAKING A PRIVATE STRUGGLE PUBLIC

There was a time, six years ago, when I did allow my private struggle with breast cancer to become public, although at the beginning I never intended that to happen.

It began with my photographer daughter, Annabel, and I deciding she would make a photographic record of my treatment and recovery. It was our completely private way of getting through it. It allowed her into the room with me so she didn't have to play the role of the person who sits out in the waiting room. And I didn't have to be the patient who comes out and tries to put a brave spin on things. Instead, she would be actually part of it; and also she would be able to look at me in distress, after surgery, after whatever, and I would become the subject of her camera's lens, which protected her to a certain extent from just freaking out: "This is your mother." For me it became a way of fooling myself into, "I'm going to the hospital and I'm going to meet Annabel and she is going to document this," which was much better than, "They're going to put this poison into my vein and hopefully stop me having cancer." I could look on it as a really interesting art project that I was a part of.

I began to really rely on the photographs as a way of viewing myself going through it. I never could bring myself to look in the mirror. I found losing my hair impossibly difficult, as an awful lot of people I have spoken to have. Also the various chemicals, drugs, and everything change your face in a way you can't quite put your finger on. You're not quite you.

I would try to be the actor: this is very interesting; remember what it feels like—but I didn't like it! Yet when I looked at Annabel's pictures, I thought it was fascinating—and, wow, it actually doesn't look too bad. I could relate to the pictures in a way that I couldn't relate to the face in the mirror. It made it so much better for me.

As I was going through this, Annabel was about to graduate from Parsons School of Design. She had been thinking that this was our private thing, and she would do something else for her senior thesis and senior show. She realized this was absorbing her so much that she could never come up with the kind of energy and emotion necessary to be able to do another whole project at the same time. So she asked me how I would feel if she started taking her work into school, and I said, "Oh, that's fine." In class, they knew it was her mother; but nobody made the connection, so they weren't thinking, "Oh, look, it's Lynn Redgrave with cancer."

To be honest, my cancer was quite advanced. Part of me was afraid that if it was known to others in the business, having cancer would hurt my career. When the *National Enquirer* outed me, I was quite terrified.

Then Annabel asked how I'd feel about having some of the photos in the senior show. For a second I was hesitant about having big prints up there with the public coming in. But she said she wouldn't put anything on the wall I didn't approve of. Then it flashed through my mind that I completely disapprove of censorship of art, and that would essentially be censorship. I trusted her and I felt this was right. I also thought, "I might not even be here next year; what am I afraid of?"

Having the photos in the show led to the *New York Times Magazine* seeing her portfolio and calling a year later to say they were doing a whole issue on health, and they'd like to do a big piece featuring her photos. That led to it becoming a book [*Journal: A Mother and Daughter's Recovery from Breast Cancer*]. Now it's been a traveling exhibition. It all developed little by little by little. The last thing we ever thought was that we could share this with people. The last thing. But it's now been six years, I'm well, and I'm busier than ever.

## LEADING BY EXAMPLE

Through it all, I've known many people who have entered "famehood" and yet have remained exemplary human beings.

When I have been in tough times, particularly times that are connected to show business, I very often think, "What would Ruth Gordon do?" Ruth was such a shining example of bravery. She was feisty until the end of her days. I admired that a lot in her.

My parents were certainly role models to me, and I enormously admire my old friend Ian McKellen, not only because he is a great actor, but also for how he changed things for gay actors. There were many gay actors who were afraid to come out because it would ruin their careers. Ian went a long ways toward making it okay. He did the brilliant thing of, right after

## Never be so busy making a living that you aren't taking time to make a life.

he publicly came out, the next film he did was about Profumo, the vilified politician who was part of this prostitution ring. It was a great marketing idea of Ian's to play this straight Lothario. The fact that he was brilliant changed things. It was clear that a gay man could play a straight man. My own father, who was bisexual or gay, couldn't come out, because in his era that was death to your career. So I have a lot of admiration for Ian and how he handled it, and how he continues to be such an advocate.

## LEAVING A LEGACY

No matter what profession you're in, you need to know what's important to you in life, what kind of legacy you want to leave. For me it's wonderful to know that with movies such as *Georgy Girl* or *Gods and Monsters* you are leaving behind something tangible. But when my daughter's and my book came out, I really felt that if I was to be under the proverbial bus tomorrow, then that was something that I would be proud about leaving behind that's timeless.

I had an agent at the time who, while admiring the book and the photographs, was thinking, "Enough, already" when I couldn't act because I was off doing a book tour. While I had once been so afraid that no one would hire me to act, now I said, "You must understand that to me this is really leaving something behind that I can be very proud of, something that has helped a lot of people."

Whether for you that comes from acting, or being a good parent or good friend, or working for causes, never be so busy making a living that you aren't taking time to make a life. ★

For more from Lynn go to
http://www.nowyoutellmebooks.com/actors.

# DAVID OYELOWO

## "Keep Your Eyes on the Long Game"

One thing David Oyelowo will never have to worry about in Hollywood is being typecast, given the lack of black Brit characters in American films. His breakthrough role was that of Henry VI in an acclaimed run for the Royal Shakespeare Company in his native London in 2001. Since crossing the Atlantic to work in film and TV, he's refused to be limited by either nationality or race, in projects ranging from the spy miniseries *MI-5* to the sci-fi studio picture *Rise of the Planet of the Apes*—including, notably, a return to his Shakespearian roots as the lead in Kenneth Branagh's film of *As You Like It*. That said, he has played (or is destined to play) some great African and African-American figures, including one of the Tuskegee Airmen in George Lucas' *Red Tails*, bluesman Muddy Waters in *Who Do You Love*, the spirited Preacher Green in *The Help* and the Ugandan Dr. Junju in the critically-acclaimed *The Last King of Scotland*.

# MAKING A LIVING

## FROM ANNIE TO HEARTACHE

Don't just turn up from the small town where you were the big fish in the little pond and expect to make it in the big city. Good looks and the fact that you played Annie in school will not get you very far in Hollywood, New York, or London. You *must* train. The people I see having success and long careers are people who, as in any profession, put in the time. There's a lack of respect for what goes into being a good actor. A lot of people just think that if you can learn lines and say them

**Good looks and the fact that you played Annie in school will not get you very far.**

without fumbling in front of a camera and you work out a lot, then you're good to go. It's not true. You may get one opportunity or two; but you will be found out quickly, and you will not have a long career. And that's at best. At worst you'll turn up in L.A. trying to find an agent, and you'll only be able to attract agents who are charlatans, and you will pay them.

Never go with an agent who asks you to pay him. That's not how it works. An agent works for you, and he or she gets a cut of what you earn because he believes in you as an actor. He believes that you will work, which is why he takes you on and works for you. If you are paying him before he's gotten you an ounce of work, it's because he don't believe you're ever going to work.

If you can go to a conservatory, such as Juilliard, do. If you can't get into a school such as Juilliard, do a ton of theater. Go to Chicago, go to New York. L.A. might not have the best theater in the world, but there *is* theater in L.A. Get a theater-based training, because then there is nothing you will not be able to do. If you go straight into television, I would argue that you tend to pick up a lot of bad habits that don't allow for a long career. In the theater, an audience will very quickly let you know if you are telling them the truth or not. And you have chance after chance, night after night, to develop the ability to tell the truth to a live audience. And if you can do that to a live audience, you can do it for the camera.

## WHAT DRAMA SCHOOL CAN'T TEACH

I can't speak for university training in other countries, but I think this is certainly true for conservatory training in the UK: There's absolutely no preparation whatsoever about the practical side of being an actor. It's theater-based training—which is the best training you can get, because if you can conquer Shakespeare, Chekhov, Miller, and these kinds of playwrights, then network shows are going to be something you can do in your sleep. But the practical side was something I had to very much learn on the job. And it was hard.

No matter how much you know that the profession is fraught with rejection and job insecurity and competition and disillusionment—and that's for successful actors!—no matter how much of that is told you before you become a working actor, you can't really comprehend the reality of it. Many people face culture shock after drama school because in school you've been playing roles that, to be perfectly frank, you won't get to play for another ten to fifteen years, if ever again. You can be lulled into a false sense of what the profession means because for three years you are doing great plays with talented actors, being taught by some of the best teachers in the world every day.

> **Acting, more than most other professions, is about on-the-job training.**

Then you graduate, and many of your talented friends can't get an agent, and the class standout who was playing Lear last week is going out for these small television roles—and is lucky to get one, because television acting probably wasn't even part of the training!

Acting, more than most other professions, is about on-the-job training.

I remember on my first TV job being confused and appalled by the fact that I had to do my last scene first. And it was an emotional scene—the confession scene at the end of the drama in which I'm meant to be bawling my eyes out. I just literally was, like, "What? That's the first scene?" And I did something that only someone as naïve as a recent drama school graduate would do. I cannot believe the audacity of it now that I'm twelve years into my career. But I said to the director, "Can everyone leave the set, please? Because I need to prepare for this emotional scene." And I could see in their faces: "What? Who is this guy who's just cleared the television set in order to prepare for his scene?" Actually, it paid dividends and was an affirmative thing, though I certainly don't recommend it to everyone who's just left drama school! But I guess it was indicative of the fact that I recognized what I needed to get there, even though I was new and green to the whole thing.

Even though you'll likely get fired if you try too much set clearing—especially in TV!—it is true that you need to know what to do to get yourself to the place of telling the truth in your scene.

## AUDITIONS: MEMORIZE NOW, SLEEP LATER

There are rules of thumb that, to be perfectly honest, I'm shocked other people don't adhere to. One of the most basic is: Do not turn up to any audition without the lines learned, even if you've just gotten the script the night before. More actors than not do just that; they turn up and read the lines off the page. That's incredible to me. Because, basically, what you want to do is transport the director to the set. You want to make him or her think, "This person has taken me from this hideous exercise of putting people through the ringer to already having the part cast, and we're ready to work together on the set." The only way to do that is to deliver the kind of performance that would be worthy of a Panavision 35mm camera. That is my number one no-brainer. You're talking about thousands of dollars in recompense for getting the job! You're very rarely going to do a job for television or film in which it's not going to be enough to pay your mortgage for three or four months. Spending four or five hours the night before, losing a bit of sleep, is worth that.

## FOREIGNNESS CAN BE A TWO-EDGED SWORD

I had one very famous director whom I went in to see, and we didn't talk before the audition. I did the scenes, and he was clearly very happy with it, as were the casting directors. And then he wanted to have a chat afterward and he heard me talking in my normal voice, complete with (what he considered to be) an accent; and he just couldn't get past it. We didn't really *have* a conversation because he kept saying, "But you're British!" I realized pretty quickly that may well have been a bridge too far for him in terms of me getting the role. And I was right; I didn't get it.

But, truthfully, I've found that the pros outweigh the cons in terms of being a British actor in America. I think there is a respect here for the theatrical tradition and the training. And to be perfectly honest, when you're going into an audition room, it's like you can do a magic trick. Because you come in talking like a Brit; and then, if you can do a good American accent, by the time you've done the scene they think, "Oh my goodness, this is an extraordinary actor!" Because within the time of transitioning from yourself to the character, you've inevitably made a bigger leap in their eyes than an American actor has to, because chances are, American actors will not deviate that far from their own accents to play the character. I know for a fact that this has played in my favor several times, because people are just agog at the fact that you can switch it up.

Also, the fact that so many Brits, Australians, Canadians, and people from Ireland have had successful careers here playing Americans has dispelled any worry. My theory is that we foreigners get paid so poorly in the theater or in the television where we come from that we're perfectly happy to have craft services and a little bit of money in our pocket at the end of the day, so we're probably a lot cheaper!

## MAKE YOUR AGENTS COLOR-BLIND

My agent in England phoned me up and said, "They want you to come in and meet for *Henry VI*." And I said, "Wow, that's great. Which part in *Henry VI*?" And she said, "Henry VI." I had no frame of reference. I knew I'd been given a great opportunity, but I had no idea I was the first black actor to be afforded that opportunity by the Royal Shakespeare Company. And I had no idea that it was going to cause as big of a stir as it did in the British press. There was a point during rehearsals when I was doing interviews with the press every lunchtime. I had to stop because I recognized that the very thing they were talking to me about—my ability to play the part—was being jeopardized by the fact that I was so tired from talking to the press that I could barely focus.

The thing I'm most proud about is that a lot more black British actors have had opportunities to play those kinds of roles since. At the time, I simply wasn't aware that those opportunities hadn't been afforded.

## SHAKE IT UP

After I played Henry VI, I began being referred to as a classical Shakespearean actor. That's a fantastic label for any twenty-four-year-old actor. But the thing I needed to do straightaway was challenge that perception. So I took a TV show, a spy show that's called *Spooks* in the UK and *MI-5* here.

When I was very young—and this was a sort of naïve audacity coming through, but it was absolutely right—I told my agents, "Put me up for things that are not race-specific."

They said to me, "But casting directors stipulate! They say they want 'young, black, twenty-two, rough around the edges,' whatever. . . ." And I said, "I'll go up for those, absolutely. But if they say 'young, white, twenty-two'—put me up for *that* role also."

Some agents actually laughed at me when I said this. I didn't go with them. I held out until I found an agent who believed in me enough to put me up for many kinds of parts. It paid off, because one of the roles he put me up for was Orlando in Kenneth Branagh's *As You Like It*, and I got it! Obviously, it played in my favor that I'd done Henry VI.

Now, I'm not saying I won't play race-specific roles. But if it's going to be a caricature, if it's going to be about being a gangster or a criminal or a stereotypical thing, then you just will not find me anywhere near it. If it's a three-dimensional character who is saying something other than "I am black" in every scene, I'll do it. It's very important to me as an actor to continue to challenge the perception of you to the audience. You've got to keep the employers guessing as well; because that's when they'll consider you for anything and everything. I remember hearing that early in Denzel Washington's career, he said to his representation, "I want you to send me all the scripts that Harrison Ford turns down. Those are the things I want to do." And it's paid huge dividends for him.

## THE LONG RUN

A lot of the acting classes I've had described to me by actors are clearly being run by charlatans. They're a scam; in fact, they make people worse actors rather than better actors. A lot of it is sort of microwave training like going to an "audition workshop" or "How to get that job in three weeks"—this fast-food nation way of trying to get into the profession. While you may well learn how to do a great two- or three-minute audition, that does not equip you for doing the job, and you will get fired. And that's worse than not getting the job! Because those people will never work with you again, and they'll probably advise other people not to work with you again.

Especially in America, with the popularization of reality television and the remuneration that those kinds of celebrities can get, that kind of thinking has crept into the acting profession. It's like the guys off *Jersey Shore* or *Dancing with the Stars* or *America's Got Talent* got a contract with so-and-so, and they were just working at McDonald's three months ago. That kind of mentality creeps into acting, but that's not how Al Pacino got to be who he now is.

Keep your eyes on the long game. It can actually be detrimental for an actor to get your biggest opportunities very early on, because you can only go down from there. You want to build up slowly. If an actor gets the lead in something straight off the bat, what usually happens is that he gains a publicist, an agent, a manager, and a lawyer. All these people surround him quickly, and it becomes about trying to sustain that instead of "You know what? That was amazing to get the lead in so-and-so's movie. Now I'm going to spend the next year trying to do supporting roles just to get my confidence up, to keep on working with great directors."

The fact of the matter is, if you do that great, big successful thing, the Hollywood machine will want you to do that same thing again and again and again. The audience only has an appetite for about three of those. Once you've given them three, they don't want to see you *ever* again. By then you've lost your opportunity to say, "I'm going to take this supporting role," because then people are already saying, "He's failed. He's no longer box office, no longer a star." You're relegated to the bin, whereas if you do that after your first success, people can tell: "Wow. Smart move. He's consciously investing in a long career." And folks in the industry tend to respect that. They will tempt you back to the bigger role. But a long-game mentality is absolutely the way to have a decent career.

## CYNICISM IS NOT YOUR FRIEND

Try to retain some wide-eyed naïveté as long as you can. Because, in all honesty, after some reality checks in this industry, it's easy to fall into cynicism and bitterness. Everyone wants you when you are hot, and they will all drop you like a hot coal when, for whatever reason, you are not as useful to them as they would like. But if you walk around carrying that, it makes auditioning difficult, and it makes doing your job on the set difficult.

I'll give you an example. On the film I've just done, they wanted a big star who is a fantastic actor to play my role. For whatever reason, they couldn't make his deal work. In the rewrites to this film, the role just kept on getting bigger, so by the time this star couldn't do the film and I was the director's next choice, the studio started to panic. This role was getting more and more significant in rewrites, and we're now two weeks away from shooting, and the star has dropped out while the director wants this unknown actor. "We've got to find another *name!*" cries the studio honcho.

This goes on and on and on—e-mails, phone calls, all of it flying across my field of vision basically saying that they don't really want it to be me. I understand it; and to be perfectly frank, I don't disagree. There's a scramble for a star, but the practical fact is that the clock runs down, and I end up playing the part.

At that point I had a decision to make. I could either go on set and be furious that some people tried to get rid of me, or I could go on that set and make them feel ridiculous for having thought of going with anyone but with me. And wisely, I picked the latter. And you know what? A week in, those very same producers were thanking me and applauding me for making more of the part than was on the page—which is what any decent actor tries to do anyway. But I made a conscious choice to use the energy surrounding the casting, which could so easily have gone elsewhere. And there were very tempting moments when the very same producers who I know for a fact were working really hard to keep me from that set were the same ones going, "Hey, I was so grateful you could join us!"

I could use that energy to become gnarled and snooty, or I could make it positive.

In all honesty, I've learned a lot of hard lessons, many in terms of jealousy being directed at me, or in

**DAVE'S KEY "RULES OF THUMB"**

- Don't take a part that you may be embarrassed for your family to see.
- Consider three things: the people involved, the part and the script. If two out of three are positives, give the part serious consideration.
- Before any audition, learn your lines, even if you get the script the night before.

**DEALING WITH CONFLICT ON THE SET**

- Before accepting the part, deal with potential problems contractually. Get what you want in writing.
- If you have apprehensions about a creative issue, make sure you're on the same page as the director, not the just the producer.
- Take it outside. In other words, have important discussions off the set, not in front of the rest of the cast and crew.

For more go to http://www.nowyoutellmebooks.com/actors

terms of my own jealousy toward other actors, or in terms of not-so-nice stuff that boils up in personalities that this very competitive industry engenders. But if you're still inspired and keen to be part of the pursuit of the truth, then none of it matters. It all fades away, especially when you're with really talented people who are all on the same page. The secret is that most people who do this would do it for free, in all seriousness. But it's a multibillion-dollar industry. Once commerce and art mix, it's an ugly marriage. That's where you'll see the worst sides of the profession come in.

## NO COASTING

If I got the lead in some kind of studio tent-pole type film, it may well be a great payday, may be fantastic exposure, may be fun—and I love action, I love getting to run around and do boy stuff. But it's never going to come close to playing Martin Luther King, just in terms of the levels of challenge, and the depths of emotion and soul-searching and research and interviewing of extraordinary people. That's the zenith. That's the absolute height of what you aspire to do. But having said that, there is never a role to which I give anything less than 100 percent of my attention and ability.

I will never coast, because I've seen actors who do; and you can tell, especially if they've done good work before. You watch them, and you can see that they don't want to be there. They're phoning it in. This job was a paycheck. I never want to be that guy.

Because I've seen actors whom I admire and aspire to be like do that, and it's so disappointing. It's so detrimental to the story, because you're watching something and you're taken out of the story because you know they're not as engaged with this as the one that gave them the Oscar and the acclamation and all the money that has made them grow artistically fat. I aspire to never let that creep in. I feel like, if I'm not going to be inspired by a part or I don't really want to be there, then I won't do it. I think it's unfair to everyone else. You know, no matter how small the budget is on any project, the people involved tend to have had to work hard just to get there. A $3 million movie arguably takes more effort to pull together than a $100 million movie. And I mean that. A $100 million dollar movie is probably because you're selling a Hasbro toy title, and it's kind of a no-brainer—absolutely, let's go. But if it's a $3 million movie about a small family in Idaho, the creative team has probably been trying to get the film together for ten years. And so I just think, "Leave it to someone who wants to be there."

## THE NO-METHOD METHOD

I am not of the Method school of thought, partly because it just doesn't seem to work for me. I cannot walk around as the character on and off set. Having said that, I did a film called *The Last King of Scotland* in which Forest Whitaker stayed in character for three months, off camera and on. And it's what he needed to do because he's such a humble, gentle man—the antithesis of Idi Amin. It was kind of awkward with Forest in character all the time, to be around him in the hotel. But he's such a lovely man that that's what he needed to do to get it to where he could perfectly produce his Oscar-winning performance. That's just not me.

For me, what works is doing the research on the character, reading the books, taking the dialect classes, reading or listening to interviews, just jamming it all into my brain, then practice, practice, practice—and let it go; and then on the day you're filming, you trust that the combination of your preparation, the other actors, the director, and being there in the costume in the right setting, hopefully, will allow the magic to happen.

Again, for me, this process is all built on theatrical training. In the theater, you tend to have a minimum of four weeks rehearsal, so you know that character back to front; and you have a muscle memory of what that character feels like so that you can walk from the wings onto the stage and be taken over by the character. And that, by and large, is how I approach film. Do the work beforehand, and do it rigorously. You'll never find someone more obsessively voracious than I am in terms of imbibing as much information as I can before I am on set; and then, by the time I'm there, there's no question in the world you will be able to ask me that I won't be able to answer in terms of the character. That means I don't feel a need to be him all the time. It's also partly because I'm very English and that just feels a little embarrassing and over the top for me. But I've been in America three and a half years now, so you never know; I may yet be persuaded otherwise.

## LEARNING TO DO MORE . . . AND TO DO LESS

The secret to a long career lies in taking the opportunity to learn from every gig you do—whether it be from the directors, the other actors, or the producers. When great actors become less exciting to watch, it's when they rest on their laurels. It's when they think they've arrived and they've surrounded themselves with yes people and they've lost sight of that hunger that produced those great performances earlier on in their careers.

Some of the worst experiences have been the ones in which I've learned the best lessons. But with every opportunity, I try to glean as much as I can. I got to play Muddy Waters in a film called *Who Do You Love*, and I had to learn to play slide guitar in three months and be able to play it live. That was an opportunity to see just how much the fear of looking stupid can produce in you: a miraculous acquisition of new skills!

On an HBO miniseries called *Five Days*, I had a director, Otto Bathurst, who got things out of me I didn't know I had inside. He kept on saying, "Less. Do less. Do less." Until that job, I hadn't fully felt the power of the camera in terms of how much is readable by literally thinking it as opposed to projecting it. That was a huge learning curve for me.

## ACTORS, UNLIKE BEGGARS, CAN BE CHOOSERS

I do believe in saying, "no" to a lot of things. For me, because I'm a Christian, having that moral compass through which things have to pass actually helps with quality control. A lot of things that are bad tend to be schlocky, in your face, low on story, high on sex—just for shock. The fact that those projects are not things I am prepared to put my name on helps.

Also, acting has never been about money for me. Yes, I have a family and a mortgage and responsibilities to meet, but I would much rather go and work in the supermarket than be on a set for six months feeling suicidal because I've prostituted myself. I genuinely would rather do that. My wife and I have had to make some very tough choices when those opportunities have come along. I've been blessed in that some of the things I've gone for, hoped to get, and didn't get were things that turned out to be things I was glad not to have gotten.

My rule of thumb is to consider three things: the people involved, the part, and the script. If two of the three are quality, it's likely a go for me. If it's one out of three, that's much more iffy. A lot of the time, it's none of those things, which makes the decision easy. But if you're offered even a small role in a great script, it is true that great writing creates great actors. You're only as good as your material, to a certain extent.

Right now, I'm arguably as successful as I've ever been in terms of work and acclaim and standing in the profession. But up until a film I just did called *Rise of the Planet of the Apes*, I had gone a year with no work whatsoever. I got to be at home with my wife and kids—which is lovely, but not what I was planning. And this fallow period came after playing one

**Acting jobs seem to inevitably follow the pattern of buses in New York City: none come at all, then six arrive at once.**

of the leads in a George Lucas–produced film, *Red Tails*, which had led me to think, "Okay, great, here we go! Playing the lead in a Lucasfilm movie, one of the Tuskegee Airmen . . . This is exactly the reason my wife and I moved to L.A.! I'll work nonstop now!"

But it coincided with a time in which a lot of studios got rid of their independent wings, so unless you wanted to be third henchman to a superhero in some terrible movie, not much was happening. As far as network television, shows are very few and far between that make you genuinely think, "Wow, this is so great that I'm prepared to risk signing a seven-year contract." Almost never do I read anything from network television that tempts me to make that decision. And a lot of cable stuff is quite dark, and, like I say, doesn't really fit within the kind of thing I want to sign my name to. So that was a tough year we've just had—that a lot of actors have had.

Acting jobs seem to inevitably follow the pattern of buses in New York City: none come at all, then six arrive at once. There have been worthy projects I've had to turn down simply because the timing clashes with another project. No matter how long you're in the business, that's one of the tougher things. You're not doing anything for months and months, and then two great roles come along at once. Thankfully, I haven't been in the situation where the one I chose went on to clearly be the wrong choice.

The most heartbreaking things I've turned down have been in the theater. After I had that wonderful run with the Royal Shakespeare Company playing Henry VI, they came back and asked me to play King John, Romeo, and Henry V. When I was growing up, I didn't know if I dared dream of those things, especially as a black actor. But it was a time to capitalize on the fact that I was gaining more of a film and television career, and it didn't make sense to commit to another eighteen-month run in the theater. I couldn't commit to living in Stratford-upon-Avon when my family had moved to the U.S. and our furniture was crossing the Atlantic. Those are heartbreaking decisions to make.

I haven't once regretted anything I've turned down for reasons other than schedule, though. Even if it's gone on to be incredibly successful, the reason for which I turned it down becomes the thing I'm reading about later. Actors' instincts tend to be right on.

## KNOW WITH WHOM TO NEGOTIATE

I had one experience that was a tricky one. It was a five-episode miniseries for the BBC and HBO called *Five Days*. When I went in to meet the producers and casting people, they only had the first three scripts. This was clearly phenomenal writing and an incredible role, and there was nothing about these first three scripts that would make me think anything other than, "I want to be a part of this."

Thankfully, I was offered the role; but then I said, "Well, it's tough for me to sign on to this without knowing what happens in the fourth and fifth episodes." They gave me an outline; but the writers were still working on it. It sounded very much in the same vein of the first three, and so I signed on.

It was only later when I got the full script for episode four that I saw it involved what seemed to be a fairly raw sex scene, which was something I had never done.

Sex scenes are not something I blanket say I don't want to do; it's all about how they're shot. A rule of thumb for me is that I don't want to do anything that I'm going to be embarrassed for my kids to see when they're of age to see the material. The way this was written, it wasn't gratuitous or out of sync with the project; but it was just not something I wanted to do as written. So I phoned the producer and said, "Look, I'm not comfortable with this scene. I understand it being there, but let's talk about how this is going to be shot." He assured me that it was going to be very tastefully done and, "It's not about seeing everything; it's more about the fact that these two people engage in this act together"—and it *was* right to see that in the show.

Now, the mistake I made was to go on the producer's word and not the director's. The director hadn't signed on yet; and when he did, of course, he wanted to make his own creative decisions. However, because I'd had a specific conversation with the producer, I assumed the issue was settled.

Fast-forward to the day of shooting the scene. The actress involved, the director, and I had lunch; and we were driving to the set. And the director started talking about how he was going to shoot the sex scene. And I was, like, "Whoa. I had a conversation with the producer and was categorically assured this scenario was not what was going to take place! This is exactly the situation I was calling to avoid."

The director didn't want to hear it. The producer had not run this by him. In fact, the director decided to turn on the emotional blackmail by saying things such as, "Artistically, this really hampers my vision, and I feel disappointed that you're going to constrict us like this."

At the same time I was thinking, "I don't care! I've done my piece, which was to make sure that I'd made my grievances known, and was sure we'd come to an agreement."

Meanwhile, the actress with whom I was doing the scene was very game. She would do anything, and that did not help my cause. So we go to do this scene, and she's meant to be topless in the scene, and I went, "Look, I want great, big Band-Aids over her nipples." Because there *is* something different once you see a lady's nipples and it's a lovemaking scene; it just goes in a different direction. Thankfully, she obliged. The director was scowling in the corner.

So we did the scene, and it's mortifying as hell; but it's within the realm of what I'm okay doing. Cut, moving on. *Whew.* But wait. The director comes up to us and says, "We saw the plasters in the shot, and there's no way to cut around it." So the actress goes, "Okay, I'll take them off," and she does. The fact of the matter is, I can legislate what I will and won't do, but I can't direct her. I can't force her to do what she is now no longer comfortable with. So the director had effectively backed me into a corner, and we ended up doing the scene again; and by the time I watched the show, that was a clear "I am never going to be in that situation again." That was a mistake.

In hindsight I should have dealt with it contractually and gotten it in writing. Another mistake I made was talking to the producer rather than to the director. If I'd talked to the director, perhaps we could have managed to reach a compromise that would have made us both happy. Certainly, the place *not* to be dealing with that is on the set, when it involves another actor, and a director who's upset about his artistic vision being compromised. I mean, the show was great and did wonderful things for me. But that situation changed the way I will approach things in the future.

There are no hard-and-fast rules, and that's why I don't categorically say "I would never do a sex scene," because I don't think in and of themselves they are wrong in terms of storytelling. It's a part of life. What I'm opposed to is when they are gratuitous, when they're for titillation, when they are done in a way that isn't tasteful or are just for the sake of shock instead of moving the story forward. I realize now it's important to have clear communication with the creative entities involved as opposed to communicating with the money. Because the money people will say *anything* to get you on that set.

# MAKING A LIFE

## BRING THE FAMILY

Successful marriages between actors are unfortunately the exception rather than the rule. Often it's because people don't lay out their priorities early in their marriages, and often because they don't realize how important it is to have a life outside of acting in order to be a good actor as well as a good spouse. If you prioritize make-believe over reality, fundamentally, you won't go very far as an actor. That's why some great actors become worse with age, because they are less and less in contact with the ruggedness of the life they had before the trappings of that success.

When my wife and I got married, we pledged that we would never be apart for more than two weeks. We just celebrated our twelfth wedding anniversary, and we've managed to stick to it. It's been difficult but incredibly rewarding. It's meant that we have a very good marriage, wonderfully happy children, and a harmonious home. And I do think we're better actors for it, because in order to keep that going, you have to deal with the thing that is an occupational hazard for the actor—which is selfishness. You cannot put your wife and children first and be selfish at the same time. You cannot be self-obsessed and make that work.

If you are able to be generous with your time, your emotions, and your spirit even in the middle of playing a role, it inevitably impacts on the role. Because

**No matter how balanced you are as an individual, being an actor does produce a particular brand of neurosis that is born out of rejection, born out of anxiety about where your next job is going to come from, and born out of being a very social animal because that's part of your job.**

the best acting and storytelling are intrinsically generous. It's not about the actor; it's about serving the story, the other actors, and the vision of the director. And if you have already said to the producers, "I will only take this job if you have me on a plane every two weeks to get back to my family," the fact that this isn't just about you and that you aren't the primary focus of your life is just in your DNA. That makes it a lot easier when you're telling a story with other people to serve the story, because I make that choice for my family, as a point of service and demonstration of love to them.

A lot of actors, without a second thought, will go off for four months and be away from a newly born baby or a new marriage. That to me is insanity. Our two-week rule is both difficult and completely impractical. But my family is living proof of the fact that, if it is your priority, it can be done. It means turning down work. It means I had a crazy situation not long ago where I was doing a film in Morocco and flying back three times in order to keep the two-week rule going—and the flying time each way was twenty-four hours. That's six times traveling all day to get back for three or four days to be with my family. But the love that grew between my wife and me in that time was exponential, because it's a demonstration of the fact that I'm not falling in love with some beautiful actress in Morocco, where I'm living it up and having *tajine* under the moonlight. I was saying, "You know you are my priority, and any opportunity I have, I'm going to get back to you, and that for me is a fundamental nonnegotiable."

I think being married to another actor makes it easier, not harder, because you understand the challenges the other faces. You understand the hours, and you understand the neurosis. And no matter how balanced you are as an individual, being an actor does produce a particular brand of neurosis that is born out of rejection, born out of anxiety about where your next job is going to come from, and born out of being a very social animal because that's part of your job. If you are an actor who is married to a preschool teacher, your hours are going to be a challenge. Your outlook on life is going to be a challenge. Your social circles are going to be a challenge. And to be perfectly honestly, things like the two-week rule are going to be a challenge. Because one of the things that we do is we travel together; and because we're both self-employed, we can make that work. We can homeschool our kids in order to make that work as well. So there are things where, practically speaking, both of you being actors definitely helps.

**Be happy. And don't forget to say thank you.**

Now, if you're two actors who have become subject to self-obsession and bitterness and all the by-products of being an actor that are easily slipped into, then your marriage may still suffer. One of the things that we said early on—and we absolutely live by—is: God first, our marriage and children second, then our profession. I would be lying to you if I didn't say those things don't shift around now and again, but the fact that in our minds that's the ideal and what we work toward is very important.

God bless the Screen Actors Guild. If you're doing a movie abroad, the producers have to get you a first-class ticket. The price of that first-class ticket will usually pay for five economy-class tickets, which means everyone can come. The production also tends to put you in fairly expensive hotels. So I go to them and say, "Tell you what; don't put me up in the Four Seasons. Give me the money, and I'll go find myself a three-bedroom apartment a little farther away, and my family is happy—thank you."

Then, you know what? Be happy. And don't forget to say "thank you." ★

For more from David go to
http://www.nowyoutellmebooks.com/actors.

## "Let Your Character Have a Big Ego, Not You."

Pauley Perrette was the first person cast for *NCIS*, and a decade into the show's blockbuster run, she's still the series' most delightfully peculiar and indelible presence. As Abby, she's ridiculously perky, a little bit punky, and easily the most loveable and brilliant forensic scientist ever to toil in a basement lab for a military law enforcement agency. Pauley's lovability has been scientifically quantified by Q ratings, which have declared for several years running that Perrette is the most popular actor on prime-time TV.

Because she shies away from the limelight and lives a fairly Spartan existence, the public doesn't really know much about Perrette off-screen. Prior to *NCIS*, she enjoyed less high-profile roles, like a bit part in the film *Almost Famous* and roles on television as Drew Carey's girlfriend or Christina Applegate's stalker. She's also an accomplished musician. But most fans don't really know if she's like Abby or not. The answer is, no, as far as pigtails and posture go, but, yes, when it comes to philanthropy and giving hugs.

# MAKING A LIVING

## NOTHING BEATS (OR IS CHEAPER THAN) AN ON-SET EDUCATION

If you're not willing to work for free, and if you're not willing to be an extra, I have nothing to say to you. Nothing! I got my SAG card from being pulled in for a bigger part when I was working as an extra. I don't know if it's humility or brilliance to know that being on a film set as an extra—or being on a film set *anywhere*—is way smarter than sitting home on your couch thinking about how great you are. I wanted to be in the middle of it. I was trying to learn the lingo, trying to learn what was going on. If somebody said to me, "It's at craft service," I thought that meant they were gluing little beads on boxes. I had no idea!

> **Being an extra and paying attention is like free acting school.**

So if I wasn't booked on something as a character, I would be throwing myself in there as an extra, just to be watching and listening and learning all the time. As an actor, you can have no fear. At the beginning my only fear existed because I didn't know the rules that made you at ease on the set. Working as an extra addressed that.

Back then, I was broke. When I worked as an extra, they would give me fifty bucks to get some food, and I would stay on set for twelve hours, happy as a clam. If you go to film school, you've got to pay. Go to acting school, you've got to pay. How can you turn down free film school? Being an extra and paying attention is like free acting school. Why would you not? Because of your ego. But there's not really any place for an ego if you want to be a good actor. Let your character have a big ego, not you.

When I hear any new actor say, "I'd never be an extra," I'm done talking to him. There's nothing else to say. I did it—proudly.

## THE GETTING IN SHAPE FOR THINGS TO COME

There's a saying for actors on the set that goes, "Never stand when you can sit, never sit if you can lie down, and never lie down if you can go home." Which is so true, because it takes a lot of stamina. I tell young actors, "Make sure you're in good shape." That's not vanity. It takes a lot of stamina to work for fourteen, fifteen, seventeen, eighteen hours on your feet, doing this kind of stuff.

It also helps you be prepared for demands you might not expect. I'm an athlete; I'm a kickboxer, I'm a runner, I try to do as many kinds of athletics as possible. But even I have been surprised by what directors want out of you.

I went in and auditioned for one role, and all I did was read a little one-page scene with just dialogue—that was it. I got hired for the job, and they flew me to San Diego. When I got there and they said, "Okay, the first day and a half will just be training," I said, "Training for what?" They said, "Kung fu." And I was like, *Really?*

I had auditioned on a one-page dialogue scene, having no idea I was playing a kung fu master. But I thought to myself: "I can do that. I'm a total athlete."

And I learned it. I'm a kickboxer, which helps. But how did they know that? They didn't ask me! It wasn't anywhere in any of the material I was given. That was a big risk on their part because it was rough, physical stuff. I mean, what if I was some prima donna, not some redneck chick from Alabama who'll do anything? They would have been screwed, completely.

## WITH AGENTS, SIZE MATTERS . . . AND SMALLER IS BETTER

Some people ask how you get an agent, and I really have no idea about the agent process at that very first stage. I started working before I had an agent.

Then, for a while, I was with a really big agency. I later moved to a smaller agency that was more selective. I would compare being with a big agency to sleeping on a metal slab in a prison. And being at a smaller agency is, to me, like sitting in a comfy recliner with an afghan blanket.

But different actors want different things. Certainly more packaging goes on at the big agencies. That's another thing about getting a job or not getting a job. You may audition and be absolutely the best actor who ever performed in front of anybody, ever, but the agency behind the production company has a packaging deal with their actors and they have to use one of them. Packaging may be a dirty word among the big agencies, but they do it all the time. And that determines who directs, who acts, who does all kinds of stuff.

Packaging and nepotism pretty much rule this town. Those things aren't going to help me. I'm with a boutique agency. And my dad's a firefighter in Alabama! And somehow I still manage to get work.

## YOU'RE NEVER JUST AUDITIONING FOR ONE ROLE

Ugh. Auditioning is the worst. And that comes from someone who gets hired a lot! I have about as high a success rate as you can get.

Keep in mind that an audition is a surreal situation, in a surreal setting. The people you read with aren't your co-actors. The room is not a set. There's nothing there. It's so weird. I have no idea how casting directors do their job.

As an actor I want to walk into an audition and say to whoever's sitting there, "Look, here's the thing: Hire me, and I will make you so proud. Whatever it takes, you will be so glad that you hired me."

I'm always so grateful to be hired that I think, "I'm going to do everything in my power to make that casting director, that producer, and every single person that had a hand in hiring me think, 'Thank God we hired her.'" It's a mission for me. I'm grateful, and I want them to be proud.

But I don't know how *they* know any of this when I walk in the door. How do they know that I'm gonna kick ass? I don't know, because auditioning is a bizarre process. Everybody hates it, I think.

When you're auditioning, be prepared. Go in there and do the best job that you can, and then know it may not be the job for you. People say to me, "Oh, you work all the time." Yes. But that sometimes means I went on fifty auditions, and got one job. But you know what? That one job you got is exactly where you're supposed to be. Don't worry about the forty-nine you didn't get! Don't think about it for a second. (Unless you went in and were a total ass. Then maybe you should consider not being an ass next time.)

You don't know what's going on. In this crazy town, it could be anything. Sometimes you lose a job because a director's niece's new boyfriend needs a SAG card. Or because the director wanted to sleep with somebody else who auditioned. Or because the director wanted to sleep with *you,* and, not so much. Or it could be because you wore a blue shirt and they hate blue. You audition, you go home—don't worry about it. Done.

**Sometimes you lose a job because a director's niece's new boyfriend needs a SAG card.**

Here's another thing to remember: They want you to be really good. There can sometimes be a feeling like you're in a gauntlet; you feel that the whole group of casting people is aiming guns at you, wanting to tear you down. But the best thing that can happen to a casting director or a director or a producer is for an actor to come in and kill it and be amazing. They don't want you to be bad! They want the same thing you do, for you to be great!

Also remember you can be great and not get the job. It's happened to a million fantastic actors. I've done auditions where I thought "Oh, I killed that—I'm perfect for it," and I didn't get it. When that happens, I believe there's always a cosmic reason why. For example, maybe it's because the week that I was supposed to be shooting that project, I would have been completely unavailable to audition for a project that I did get that was way better.

You can't plan the future. We don't know what all of it means. Have faith.

Here's another thing I tell actors. No matter what the role is—even if you get called in to audition for something and you're thinking, "I'm not really right for this," or if it's something where they already have somebody picked out—go in dedicated to doing your absolute best. Every time. Casting directors and directors and producers are not just around for one day or one project. You can go in and be brilliant in a role that you're not right for; you can be the wrong race or wrong height or whatever. But they're making notes, not only for that project, but for the next ten projects.

**[Casting directors] are making notes, not only for that project, but for the next ten projects.**

That has happened to me so many times, where I've gotten a call and the casting director has said, "You auditioned for [blank] way back, and they couldn't hire you for that, but they loved you and want to bring you in for this." Thank God I went in there prepared—because it created a memory for them. They're keeping track of *everything.* Never go in there and blow one off, because they're going to put that down in their book of "not good."

## LOVE THY CREW AS THYSELF

I find that the most talented actors are the nicest. It doesn't have anything to do with whether they're famous or not famous, or how big they are. Actors who aren't very good are usually the worst to the crew, and the worst to work with. I don't know if that's a cast-in-stone rule, but it has been in my experience. You get some hack on the set, and he's the one demanding stuff and being rude to the crew. Then you work with a brilliant actor with genius talent, and she's easygoing and fine. I don't know if it's connected to insecurity. Do bad actors know they're bad? There's a question for the ages!

My number one piece of advice is always: respect your crew. Because no matter how cool you think you are, they're there hours before you are, and they'll be there hours after you leave. Every single part of this machine has to work together, and to treat your crew with the utmost respect, with complete humility on the actor's part, is so important.

Often when civilians—people who aren't in the entertainment industry—come to the set, one of the things that surprises them the most is how many people it takes to make a TV show or film. It's hundreds of people. And I've seen an entire production taken down by one person being a jerk. It can ruin the temperature of the set.

Back in the '20s and '30s, they had all these protocols for the set. Such as, if you were on the crew, you were not supposed to talk to the actor, or even look at the actor. That doesn't make any sense, because everybody's working together. Actors can do whatever they want to do, but if somebody's not shooting and lighting it, nobody's going to see it. Those rules may not exist anymore, but I think there's something still left over of that in the DNA of film and television, where there's some sort of weird thing about the actors being on another level. And because of that I think it's even more important that the actors are super-respectful of the crew, and humble and grateful, at all times, for everything that they do.

I always say: Serve your project, not yourself. If everybody's point is to make the project the best it can be, there will be no egos involved, because everyone is working together as a means to the same end. If in going from point A to point B, your point B is to stroke your own ego, then you're not serving your project. If your point B is to maintain some kind of hierarchal B.S. about who's more important than the other person, it doesn't work.

**Serve your project, not yourself.**

## DON'T STUDY OTHER ACTORS TOO MUCH

There are times when I've heard an actor remark, "Gee, I know who *your* hero is." It's obvious when an actor is imitating another actor's portrayal of somebody. I would never name names, but I could tell you ten actors right now, where it's, "Oh, he loves Nicholson." Or, "That guy loves De Niro—hello!" But that's not Robert, and that's not Jack; that's Bob or Jack's portrayal of a character that you're imitating. You don't know what those guys are like at home!

## DO STUDY OTHER PEOPLE . . . AND PETS

I have no acting training. I didn't go to film school. But I've found having degrees in sociology, psychology and criminal science has helped me immensely as an actor, because I studied human behavior as a science—which is what acting is.

I would never say that anybody's path should be the same as mine. But I have seen people who get caught up in being professional acting-class takers. That's what their life becomes about. And I've thought, "Wow, it might be good to step out of your acting class and just go live. Walk around, listen to people, watch them in their sorrow and their glory." Because every time you're given a character, it's your responsibility to represent them fairly, to know who they are and what they're about, just as if you were testifying for them in court.

**Walk around, listen to people, watch them in their sorrow and their glory.**

Someone once said, "Never befriend a writer, because you'll be involved in the story they're creating in their head." You could say that about me as an actor. Don't think that anyone or anything that crosses my path of consciousness is not being studied.

I had an encounter the other day with a woman who was saying some very strange things to me, and the people around me were sort of nervously sucking in their breath. Afterward, they were like, "Oh, sorry that happened." And I was like, "Wow, you know what? I would love to play her!" I was studying her, as she was being really weird. I was like, "Huh. Okay—so *that's* how that kind of brain works." And I'll end up playing her, at some point. I'll remember her.

People's body language—the way they sit, the way they talk, everything they do—is connected to something. It's fascinating. I can look at strangers any time and pick up something I can use. I do it almost all the time, without even meaning to. If somebody called me tomorrow and said I had to play that guy who I saw sitting in a booth at the restaurant I was in tonight, I would know how he holds his fork. And how he sits—and does he lean in, or does he lean out? Is he smiling, and/or are his eyes smiling? I'm watching. I've used my niece for a lot of stuff. She's now eighteen, but watching her grow up, I've seen lots of little discoveries and mannerisms she's had. I've played her in several things.

I have a friend who can't inhabit his character until he has his costume on. My thing is that I have to figure out a character's *gait*. Does she walk fast or slowly? Does she stand upright? When I get that, I'm off and running—pun intended. There are reasons for the way we hold our bodies, and sociologically and psychologically, it's fascinating to put all those things together. I'm observing everybody—every single crew member, everybody I see. There'll be a guy at the market and I'll watch him, thinking, "Huh! I wonder how that happened. How did he end up with that gait?"

On *NCIS*, Abby stands like she's very alert and direct. I'm very slouchy. She and I are totally different in that way. I could just curl up in a ball in flannel at any moment and be totally happy. Abby's very pristine. She's clean. She's buttoned up. Everything's perfect in her lab. Abby would never roll out of bed in the shirt she slept in and show up to work. I do that all the time.

I am totally into being comfortable and no nonsense. I'm rarely not in sneakers, old jeans, and delicious, yummy clothes that are often not that clean. I don't care! Unless I have to go to an event or photo shoot, and then I have to clean up nice, which I do.

Here's another tip: study your pets. The way Abby walks, the way she stands, the way she cocks her head, the way she interacts with stuff, how she reacts when she gets confused or excited—everything about her is based on my dog, a rat terrier-Chihuahua mix. I have played her as my dog since day one. Abby's ponytails are even based on my dog's ears!

## BEING AN ON-SCREEN ROLE MODEL

On *NCIS*, Abby's never called herself "Goth." Everyone else does. I don't mind that viewers think of her as Goth. People should understand that there are many sides to everybody, and those dynamics are a good thing.

When I first got this job, people kept asking me: Where did this character come from? So I interviewed Don Bellisario, who created the character. He said he's always loved taking on stereotypes. Back when he created *Magnum P.I.*, he thought that the images of Vietnam veterans in the media were mostly negative, so he wanted to create a character who was a Vietnam veteran who was figuring it out, moving on, and doing well. It was the same sort of thing when he created Abby. He thought the "alternative" group of young people were usually represented in the media as junkies and thieves, so he wanted to write a super-alternative character who is an uber responsible, brilliant scientist—and goes to church! And it's changed perceptions all over the world.

I hear from girls all over the world, saying they started watching *NCIS* when they were eleven or twelve and now they're going into college and pursuing math and science. They call it the "Abby Effect." It's a pretty amazing phenomenon for a fictional TV character to actually change people's lives.

# MAKING A LIFE

## BEING AN OFF-SCREEN ROLE MODEL

While Abby's a great role model, I'm as flawed and as strange as anybody else. The only advice I give with confidence is this: volunteer and give back, because I believe that's what we're here to do. We're all going to struggle and have hard times, so it's important to fill others up when you're having a good day.

I'm completely charity-driven in my own life. That's what I do with my free time; I work for thirty charities. And my producers and the network have been unbelievably kind in continuing to incorporate my personal charities into the show. Abby did something with Habitat for Humanity, which I worked for as a teenager. We had a Seeing Eye dog episode that featured Petfinders.com, which is a wonderful animal adoption website. We've had storylines that have incorporated Save the Children, Doctors without Borders, and the American Red Cross. The producers have been great.

I recently told one of my producers, Charles Johnson, that I honestly believe charity is part of why *NCIS* has been such an unbelievable, historic success. To have twenty million viewers every week in our ninth year—I don't know if that trajectory has ever happened before, where a show reaches that point after so many years of rising. I would like to believe that part of that has to do with how much the cast and crew believes in giving back. It is a set full of incredibly generous, philanthropic people. There's not a single day where one of our crew members isn't getting a hat signed for an auction for their charity, or something in that vein. In nine years, there've been millions of dollars raised for charity through the people that work on NCIS. I don't know if I'd call it karma, but it's got to come back somehow. How could it not?

## STUFF

I've always been a minimalist. If somebody was to break into my house— which they won't, because I have an alarm system and cameras and everything else—they would be so disappointed. Because I don't really own anything. Somebody tried to give me an iPad, and my computer is so old that it doesn't even recognize it. Likewise, my station wagon is so old, I was sitting in traffic today and I had a guy yelling through the window: "Hey, are you Pauley Perrette?" I was like, "Yeah, dude." And he's like, "That's your car? Why are you driving that?" "Because I like it." It's a good car. I don't need a fancy one.

I don't wear jewelry. People give me something and I'm like "Uhh . . ." I don't know what to do with it. There's absolutely nothing materially or monetarily that I want. A cold beer is good! I don't know what other actors do—I guess they go to spas and buy jewelry and designer clothes, and that probably is a great sense of joy for them. So I know the feeling. But that's the way I feel when I'm able to donate an amount of money to Project

Angel Food and know exactly how many people that is going to feed that are homebound with cancer or AIDS. That's my jewelry.

> **Being able to shine a light on my causes is the only thing that I like about being famous.**

I've always been a volunteer. Even when I was a bartender in New York, when I was broke, I gave as much as I could. I've said before and I'll say it again: Being able to shine a light on my causes is the only thing that I like about being famous. Everything else about it is dehumanizing. But that is huge. Even though I'm doing and saying the same things, nobody would have cared when I was a bartender. For whatever reason, they listen a little more now.

## FROM TWITTER-PHOBIC TO TWITTER-HOLIC: HOW ACTORS CAN HARNESS SOCIAL MEDIA

When I first got on Twitter it was to help save a women's shelter. And it worked. We saved it, and that was amazing. Right now we're raising a lot of money for AIDS Walk through Twitter. You can also use Twitter to spread a little hope and joy. Just the other day, a Bible verse in Psalms helped me so much. It says, "God saves the broken hearted and saves the spirit of those who are crushed." So I tweeted that. It became my most re-tweeted tweet. I heard from lots of people who said, "Wow, that's exactly what I needed to hear today." That's the magic of it.

But social networking can be also dangerous. One cost of being a celebrity is that I have some dangerous people in my life. I have restraining orders. Things like that make you realize you're incredibly vulnerable. You can have a thousand wonderful people who are your fans, and then there are two or three psychopaths. Unfortunately there are tragic Hollywood stories to prove that. I was told by the police that they didn't want me on Twitter! They said, "Okay, if you're going to do it, here are the rules." And rule number one is: You never say where you're going; you only say where you've been.

Some of my Twitter followers get mad. They say, "Why won't you reply to me? Why won't you follow me?" Unfortunately there are balls and chains that come along with being a public figure, and part of that is that I have to be completely security-driven. So my thing is I have to talk in monologues. Sometimes I'll get the same question a million times, and then I will tweet one thing that says, "No, Abby does not wear nail polish." But it's not safe to get into a relationship with people you've never met. People think they know you because they watch the show and the character. And some people form unhealthy attachments to people that they don't know. It can be very, very frightening. I just always hope that the fans understand and respect that. It's not like anybody's being mean or dismissive. It's just the rules of the game.

I can't imagine anybody having nicer fans than I do. But I also made boundaries on Twitter from the very beginning: This is a no-negativity zone, and if anybody has a negative comment about anything, you're blocked, immediately. You're not in this party. My Twitter place is a very positive, amazing place, which is pretty great, considering the fact that it's Twitter.

But it's also the fact that I don't play games. And I advise other actors to do the same. If somebody writes something that upsets you, block 'em. Done. They can go off in the universe and do whatever they're doing, but I don't have to read it. The same thing with real life. If I'm at a bar and somebody is being negative, I'm not going to stand there and hang out with that person. Just walk away.

I'm very involved in anti-bullying campaigns and anti-8 and all that. At the end of the day, even if somebody has been mean to you, I still think it feels better to be the person who's never bullied anyone. I mean, come on, I was a little, skinny kid who wore blue glasses and an eye patch and leg braces. That wasn't fun. But I've never been mean to anyone in my life. I'd rather be me, definitely.

**TWITTER RULES**

- Use Twitter to spread hope and joy.
- Support your causes.
- Make Twitter a no-negativity zone.
- Never say where you are going.
- Only say where you have been.
- If someone writes something that is upsetting, block them.

For more go to http://www.nowyoutellmebooks.com/actors

I was against social networking for so long. It sounded like a pain in the ass and, like, one more thing to do. And now, I'm a Twitter-holic. I'm on there all the time. It has been so empowering. Before, the only thing anybody knew about me was how the press decided to present me to the public that day. Twitter gives the power back to me. If something's reported about me incorrectly, I can immediately say to hundreds of thousands of people, "No, *this* is the truth, coming directly from me."

Even if an interviewer records what you say, I don't think there's ever been an article that got all the facts right. Ever. So if I say on my Twitter page that I'm single, it's because I'm trying to combat the fact that it says on the Internet that I'm still married, when I haven't been married for years. But people come back to me and say, "You're married!" Really? You're going to believe something you read on the Internet when I just said straight up, no I'm not? Nothing on the Internet is true except the time and the date— sometimes. The weather is hit or miss. But some reporters will take what I say in an interview, and mix it in with stuff that they've pulled off the Internet. And I'm thinking: "I was sitting right in front of you! Why didn't you simply ask me before you put erroneous facts out there?"

But that's what's great about Twitter. As wary as I was about it, having your own, authentic voice being heard is a wonderful thing.

And sometimes, you can save a women's shelter. Change a little corner of the world. ★

For more from Pauley go to
http://www.nowyoutellmebooks.com/actors.

# MICHAEL O'NEILL

## "Get in the Water with the Role"

**M**ichael O'Neill is instantly recognizable to almost anyone who watches television or goes to the movies—but not quite so recognizable that you spend more than five seconds wondering where you know him from before you totally buy into his role. He's perhaps best known for playing a Secret Service agent on *The West Wing*—a years-long gig that started as just one day of work. Although he usually plays authority figures, he went against type and played an unhinged gunman in the arc that unforgettably ended the sixth season of *Grey's Anatomy*. More recently, he played a folksy, amiable, high-level government agent who's revealed to be a careerist killer in a critical two-part episode of TV's top drama *NCIS*.

# MAKING A LIVING

## GATE-CRASHING AND CREATIVE ALTERNATIVES

The first question every young actor wants to ask is, "How do I get an agent?" Essentially, "How do I get into the business?" The thing is, pathways into acting careers are like snowflakes. Your way of getting in is going to be different from the way that I got in and from the way the person who's sitting next to you gets in. It's the nature of the beast. This is not a business where if you do "W", "X", and "Y", then "Z" is necessarily going to follow.

There are a couple of approaches you can take. The first is to try to get an agent or a manager to see you. Then work your way up to a casting associate, then the casting director; then try the next level, the director, the producer, the studio execs. You're basically storming the gates, which are put there to minimize the number of people who are going to get access. You can spend a career doing that, and you might get good at it.

But what I suggest at this point—because the industry is changing so fast—is to create your own work. Find projects and stories and other artists that interest you. Concentrate your time there and watch how quickly those gates fall away, become less important, or open unexpectedly.

A good example is what Charlie Day did. He got together with three or four friends and said, "What if you put several guys in a neighborhood bar, and the bar's really struggling, and they come up with increasingly elaborate schemes to keep it open?" With a minuscule amount of money they created and shot *It's Always Sunny in Philadelphia* with a digital camcorder, and sold the idea to Fox. They created an entirely new model of selling a show. In fact, Fox recently held a competition for other filmmakers to shoot a pilot on the skinny, with the promise that Fox would give a production contract to the best one. It was all based on what those guys did with *Sunny in Philadelphia*, which has become one of the most downloaded shows ever. And, creatively, they're having a blast.

Another example is a small film I did called *A Quiet Little Marriage*. A group of a actors, producers, and a director got together and fashioned a story after a germ of an idea they had. They began to meet and discuss and improvise and then write off of that exploration. The resulting film ended up winning the audience award at the Austin Film Festival and got picked up by a major cable movie network. This director and these actors created that film out of nothing, and it's a lovely little film. It can be done.

When I was in college, one of my economics professors used to say, "If the railroads had remembered that they were in the transportation business and not just the railroad business, they'd have a different market share today." Likewise, we actors need to remember we're in the storytelling business, not just the acting business.

The film industry has changed considerably since I started. It is now made up of corporate entities, which are pretty much owned by five corporations. And, in this structure, actors are labor, and the corporate business model calls for paying labor scale. But when they do that, they're saying, "We don't care if you just got off the bus or you have twenty-five years of experience; if you're not above the line [the creative heavy-hitters in a movie budget, which include the director, producers, screenwriter, casting director and stars], we're going to pay you as little as is legally permitted."

Sometimes you can fight that, and occasionally you'll win, but only occasionally.

When I started in the industry, an actor's experience and contributions to other films was considered, and you were paid accordingly. Even today, elsewhere in the corporate world, compensation goes up commensurate to experience and responsibility, but in the acting corporate world, that formula no longer applies. While there's no guarantee that any actor will "make it," there used to be a tacit understanding that if you were talented and became successful, with an impressive body of work, you could earn a living. That's no longer the case.

Why is this important to a young actor starting out? Because it's going to impact how you stay in the game. If you're going into the business to be rich or to be loved, be careful! The likelihood is, even if you're successful, you'll end up driving the old Honda, not the BMW.

So what do you do, where do you find your self-worth? I'd suggest in the only areas you can control and invest in: your community and your craft.

It's essential, and I mean *essential*, that young actors build a community. It's how information flows. ("Did you hear about this project?" "Did you hear about that call?") More importantly, you'll need somebody to share the spaghetti with, someone to cover a shift, help you with a scene, or buy you a beer when your agent calls and says they went another way. So when you find people that you like being with, *be* with them. Create with them. Read plays with them. Do improv. Do rehearsals. Creatively, and otherwise, they'll save your life.

> **It's essential, and I mean essential, that young actors build a community.**

As for craft, your goal is to become so good they can't not hire you. Hit it and hit it hard.

They'll be times when things are as dead as a hammer, and if you sit, you'll fold up into a very small package. Learn a poem every day. Write. Study paintings in a museum. Go to lunch with someone and, in the middle of it, do an emotional preparation of someone with a sore tooth until your friend says, "Are you all right?" Work on a character you'll probably never be cast as. Find a Bill Esper or a Larry Moss or a Patsy Rodenburg or an Ellen Geer and trust your instrument to them. I could barely read aloud when I started. I had a lot of help along the way.

So the quest to find an agent can be a little like chasing fool's gold. Not that it's not important to have good representation; it is. But we set these things up for ourselves, like: if I can get an agent, I'll start being seen, if I start being seen, I'll start working, when I start working, people will realize my brilliance; when they realize my brilliance, a star will be born. But cause and effect are not givens in the business, in my experience. The business is indifferent to you, neither for nor against your talent and your accomplishments. And I'm not just talking to new actors trying to get in; it's indifferent to its seasoned veterans. You're nothing but labor and product to them, and I daresay that none of us started in this business to be product.

## HAVE A PLAN B . . . AND EXERCISE IT
### (WHAT DO YOU DO ABOUT THAT CORPORATE MODEL?)

When I started, I turned down a lot of "regular" jobs outside the business because I was afraid that if I engaged with that job, I would be pulled away from acting and I wouldn't come back. I was like a dog with a stick; I just wasn't going to let go. I was fortunate that I started at a time that if you held on long enough and you created a presence and got opportunity and showed up for that opportunity and did a decent job, more opportunity would follow.

The level of young talent that is coming in today is unbelievable. It's like what Julius Irving or Michael Jordan did with the basketball. They played above the rim, they changed the scope of the game. But now it just takes so much more gumption to stay in the acting game, and more inventiveness.

Above all else, you can't afford to let people or corporations who know less about you than you do define your worth. That's why community and craft—and I'll add this: an alternative way of making a living—are so important. Find a plan B.

Have two things you can do that creatively engage you: acting and something else. If it's getting harder to make a decent livelihood purely as an actor, you're going to have to have something that augments your career and, more importantly, gives you a creative outlet. Even when you're working as an actor, there are long down periods of not being engaged with a project. There needs to be something that keeps your vitality and attention going. In the absence of that, having nothing to do but sit around and wait is not only expensive, it's really hard on a person. Acting is a better gig when you're not totally dependent upon it.

## AUDITIONS FROM BOTH SIDES NOW

Here's a piece of advice I give any actor: beg, borrow, or steal your way into an audition in which you can sit on the same side of the table as the people who are doing the casting. You'll see actors that come in to audition, and apologize for being there. You'll see actors that come in who really don't want the job—not because they think they're too good; they don't want the job because they're afraid of it. They're afraid of being *seen*. And, you'll see actors that come in do their job simply and effectively and move on.

> **Beg, borrow, or steal your way into an audition where you sit on the same side of the table as the people who are doing the casting.**

It's a marvelous thing to sit on the other side of the audition table because you find out that *it's not about you*. I've been there and seen how sometimes the best audition doesn't get the job because that actor doesn't meld with the project. They may not be the right choice with another actor who's already been cast or for the director's particular vision. As an actor, you can watch someone else's audition and think, "Oh my gosh, what they just did was stunning—but it's not right for this production." Having said that, a good audition is never wasted. You may not get that job, but it will always lead to something.

Sometimes the great difficulty is that the more you want the role, the easier it is to trip yourself up. You literally squeeze the sawdust out of the end of the bat. When you feel that happening, it's important to relax, open up your hands a little bit, and let it come to you. Sometimes I'll tell myself this may be the only time I ever get to breathe life into this character, so let's have some fun, live it out fully, see if something surprises me in the audition.

If I can do that, I can walk out of the room clean. Having said that, I can tell you, the more you wanted it, the harder it hurts not to get it. At the end of the day, it's not something that you built, or a painting you painted—it's you. It's *you* they're talking about when they say, "No, I don't want that."

I walked into an audition room yesterday, and they couldn't have been more indifferent to me. I was ready to bite through my steering wheel when I got back in my car. But it's the nature of the beast that you live to fight another day. Because I've also walked into rooms where they've physically *leaned forward*, just for the pleasure of experiencing what I had to offer.

In the audition process, the one thing I say to young actors is make sure you understand it's *your* audition. It doesn't belong to the producers; it belongs to you. So go in, take your best shot, and get out. You don't want to leave them wanting less; you want to leave them wanting more. But know that it's your room, and go in and take it. Then leave. I'd much rather have them stop me at the door than have them think, "How are we going to get him out of this room?"

## FEAR OF THE DARK

Here's one of the biggest things that I've learned in the last few years: I always thought that I had to know how to do any role before I got it, and it's not true. What I have to do is get in the water with the role and the role will teach me. As an actor, it was huge for me to understand that I will find what I need because I have to, and that the role will guide me and take me there. It sounds like a simple thing and I'm sure they teach you that in acting school—I just missed that day!

It happened with *Grey's Anatomy*. I did this big, four-part season finale, playing a widower who's on the loose in the hospital with a gun. I had so much resistance to doing it. It was far and away the darkest, most unpredictable character that I've ever played, but also the character that was in the most pain of any character that I'd ever played. He was irretrievably broken. The notion of living there for a long period of time really scared me. Moreover, as an actor, I thought, "What do I want to lend my voice to? What's my responsibility here?"

The role was about as far as you can get from the types of characters I usually play. People who have an expectation of who I am and what I can do see me as a trustworthy, solid, reliable figure that can handle authority and will step into a situation and deal with crisis management. This was utterly in the other direction. This character's actions are unredeemable. There is no scenario in which it is justifiable for a person to walk into a business or hospital and take out his inability to handle his emotions with a gun. One of the great tragedies in our society is how often this happens. We can't help but wonder, is it even possible to see the signs? Are there clues that have been given before somebody opens up with a 9 millimeter? Is there anything that can be done to intervene? I wish I had a better answer for that. A member of my family was murdered, which was one reason that even the concept of that role was so costly to me. Because families never recover from something like that. They just don't. They learn and relearn ways to deal with it, they have to go on, but they never get over the absence of that loved one. There's nothing redeemable about it.

I came within a whisper of turning down the part. When the show's creator, Shonda Rhimes, first described it to me, I said, "I don't know if I can do this." The first problem, superficial as it sounds, was my ego. My image is as the voice of authority—the guy that you can trust to solve problems, not a guy that comes in to create problems. But the bigger problem was having had a personal experience with this kind of crime and seeing what it did to my family. How do I bring all that back up? How do I engage it in a way where *I'm* that person?

I was also fearful about "monkey see, monkey do," knowing that there are unbalanced people out there.

But my wife said, "Michael, I don't know if you can turn it down. A lot of really good actors have played very despicable characters." She talked about Al Pacino in *Scarface* and—not that I'm in this league—Anthony Hopkins in *Silence of the Lambs*. I've worked with Al, and I can assure you that he entertained some doubt and shadow about going into that character. I'm sure Mr. Hopkins had some pause about Hannibal Lecter, as well.

Finally I called Shonda back and said, "I don't want it Hollywood-ized. I don't want it to become some action/adventure thing." And she said "Oh gosh, no; it's quite the opposite." And I said, "I won't point a gun at a child." And she said, "Absolutely not. There's a moment when you pass the pediatric ward and it scares us, but pointing a gun at a child isn't part of this." I continued to talk about how fearful I was of what we were considering, and she listened to me and finally she said, "Michael, I'm afraid, too." That was the moment I engaged in the project. I thought, "Okay, we're on the same page. There's an opportunity here, and I have to trust that we'll be responsible about this and not glamorize it but make it about the humanity of a man that's that broken."

When I began playing the role, I was surprised by some of the unexpected turns that it took. I was surprised with the conflict that I would feel. I was surprised that I stopped being able to sleep. I was surprised that I would start being afraid for my own family—all things that the character was going through. It was an extraordinary journey for me, but when I took the first footfall, I had no idea where that road would lead creatively.

There've been other roles that had unexpected effects on me. In *Seabiscuit*, I played a father who could no longer afford to care for his son. I didn't expect the profound sense of loss that I felt from me giving my son away. It woke me up in the middle of the night for about six weeks after those scenes had been shot. The rest of the cast and crew had moved on, and I hadn't. I was caught in a cycle.

It's the untold cost of acting, I guess.

Be as honest a human being as you can be when playing a role. What will surprise you, if you're lucky, is what playing the role does to you. I used to think as an actor that I'm doing the part; what I'm finding out is that the part's doing me. And, if I can trust my instincts, I'll be all right.

# MAKING A LIFE

## FAMILY, AS INSPIRATION AND SALVE

A really interesting thing happened during the filming of the *Grey's Anatomy* role: I couldn't talk to my girls. I'd talk to my wife some about it, but I couldn't talk to my kids. They weren't of an age that I could have a conversation about it that wouldn't frighten them. I started that role in February and I finished the last day of May, and so I would be on for eight or nine days and then off for a while, but I was living with it for a long time.

And the further that I went into the role, the bigger the wound became. It got to the point that I would sit in our home with the thousand-yard stare going. I wasn't there. I was somewhere else. Occasionally one of my daughters would walk by and just put a hand on my shoulder. I don't even think they knew what they were supporting. They just knew their dad was hurt, and it was the tenderness of that expression, just to say: "We're with you, Dad. We know you're off in space somewhere, but when you come home, we're here."

> **Don't cheat yourself out of a family. It'll be your greatest resource.**

That's been the greatest joy to me of it all. Whether or not I get a job, or whether they like me in the audition, whether or not I was good in a scene—whatever it is, when I come home, I'm still the same to my girls. I'm still Dad. Don't cheat yourself out of a family. It'll be your greatest treasure.

My family is my creative source. There's nothing that I draw from as an actor that isn't rooted in the immediacy of how valuable they are to me. In fact, most often the question is, "How do I leave the house to try and go to work?" I'm really curious about what Annie's drawing, or I hear Molly humming something or learning a poem, or I hear Ella singing and playing the piano, and I just want to stay. I'm lucky as an actor, because that stuff goes with me. They're my muses. I'm a much, much better actor since I had a family.

That doesn't mean it isn't hard sometimes, when I've got to get them to a class, but I also have forty minutes to prepare six pages of the scene. The juggling aspect of it is tricky. But that part is hard for everyone—I don't think it's unique to my profession.

One problem for me is that because there's such a childlike aspect to acting, I have to make sure that my inner child isn't in conflict with their needs. Sometimes it's not good to be my age and acting four. I'm lucky in that I married well. The fact that my wife is well-grounded is important. More than one night, she's had to say, "I've been trying to get the girls to sleep! I just got them quiet, and you're getting them all stirred up again, bouncing on the bed." Oh. Oops.

> **An actor's currency is humanity. And that's not a bad currency to share with your children.**

There's a wonderful quote that says, "Artists live on the same island as everybody else, just closer to the mouth of the volcano." Sometimes fatally so. I think the positive aspect for my kids about me being an actor is that they see me engaged and alive. Whatever it is, good, bad, or indifferent, they're seeing the whole color spectrum of it. An actor's currency is humanity. And that's not a bad currency to share with your children.

## LUCK AND COURAGE

I was thinking about something that Alan Alda said when I did *The West Wing* with him. He said, "Above all else, be lucky." Now luck can be a lot of things. And luck favors the prepared. It's not haphazard. It's just this: when you get close to the intersection of luck and opportunity, show up.

Some jobs cost more to do than they're ever going to pay financially. And you have to know that for yourself as an actor. If it's not right for you, then open your palms, release it, and let something else come in. I turn down the role of racists. I just won't play them. I grew up in the South. I lived through the turmoil and the injustice of that time. That's not a place where I want to lend my voice, because it's history for me, and I don't want to go back there by playing that role. It would cost me more to be that character than they could ever offer; they haven't printed enough money yet.

Usually if I turn something down, it's just not something that I can get a shoulder behind. I can't find a way in to be able to contribute, and I can dig and dig, but on some level I don't believe in it or I'm not galvanized or challenged by it. So much of what actors do is based on confidence. If there's something that so steals your confidence that it's going to take too much time to get back on the balls of your feet, let it go. Move on to the next one. Trust there'll be a next one. That's the biggest thing.

The other thing is, be willing to make mistakes. George Bernard Shaw said, "Every stroke of genius is a lucky misreckoning." There's a tendency to feel you must do it *right*. That mind-set removes the

> ## I wish I would've been more willing to embarrass myself.

possible wild-card of the mistake. In the theater, audiences love mistakes. They'll almost always applaud a mistake. And, hey, it's only film. If it's a terrible mistake they can go back and get another take. But to relish those mistakes, that's taken me a long time. For many years, I was so busy trying to do it right that I missed mining the wonderful minerals that might've been truly interesting. I wish I would have been more willing to embarrass myself.

## BEYOND LAW ENFORCEMENT

You need to know what your toolbox looks like. They never hire you for what you can't do; they always hire you for what you can do. If your bearing is that of authority and that's what they need, then you know what to go after—and there are a lot of roles for authority figures. There's always going to be the president of the university, there's always going to be the

FBI, there's always going to be that element—but it's only an element. When the opportunity comes to play a different sort of part, I really try to invest there. When *Seabiscuit* came along, I'd come off playing Butterfield on *The West Wing*, who as a Secret Service agent was the ultimate authority or protection—a guy who wears an earpiece and a pistol and is willing to take a bullet to save another man's life at any given moment, 24/7. To go right from that to *Seabiscuit*, I knew I had a wonderful opportunity to play something a lot closer to who I am personally than that authority figure. (I'm pretty goofy, so the notion of me being an authority, my wife can tell you, is fairly amusing.) Make the most out of opportunities to mix it up. They will broaden not just your castability but your entire engagement with, and connection to, being an actor.

**You relish the times you get to come out from behind the curtain and be the wizard.**

On the other hand, sometimes you'd rather turn down a part that is very like those you've just played—and sometimes, you can. But sometimes the dictates of life pop up: What bill is coming? Who needs braces? And you need to say, "Yeah, I'll play that; I know how to wear that hat. I'll do the best job I can." But you relish the times you get to come out from behind the curtain and be the wizard.

What parts do I enjoy most? I love playing fathers because that's the main thrust of my life right now. And darker characters are always the most interesting to play—the most savory, for an actor—because they're so complicated. They're wounded, and either the cover-up or the reveal of that wound is compelling. But you know what? I really want to do one where I get the girl. That's my goal. I need an advocate, somebody willing to

**I need an advocate, somebody willing to take a risk and let me take out the earpiece, put down the gun, and try to go get the girl.**

take a risk and let me take the earpiece out, put the gun down, and try to go get the girl. When I was playing the wheelchair-bound Ron Cheals on *The Unit,* I always hoped that they would write a love scene for him and his wife. She'd left him for a while because of his drug abuse, and I always thought the tenderness of that reconciliation would be compelling. He was a man that had been cut down in his prime, but that battle-scarred warrior had a hunger in him that I always wanted to explore. He wanted to get the girl and so did I.

## LET'S GET SMALL

Let me give you this story. I hadn't worked in a while. I'd done an episode of *Jag* in February and then, nothing. I couldn't get thrown in jail. My wife was pregnant with the twins, so she had to stop working in May. There was no money coming in. My agents called in August after a very long, tenuous time. I mean, I looked like a cat on a screen door by then, the way I was just hanging on. And they said, "There's a character in *The West Wing,* Butterfield, a Secret Service guy—we want you to come in on it, but it's only one day." I answered, "Get out of here. Do you have any idea how good the writing is on that show? I'm not burning that show [i.e., losing the chance to later play a meatier character] for one day of work. I'm not doing it." And I'm thinking, "This is what it's come to after twenty years? One day on a TV show? This is all I can get? I should go see if I can buy a little farm somewhere and grow cucumbers and make goat cheese because this isn't working out so well." I don't know of any actor that hasn't come to that point at one juncture or another.

My agent said, "Michael, you need the money. Go in." So I went in and read it, and I stumbled through the first part of the audition because I had a real resistance to it. The director of that episode was kind enough to give me some notes on what I was doing wrong and give me another chance, and they called a couple of days later and said they wanted me to play the part. When I got to the set, I saw John Spencer, who I'd done a play with at Yale and with whom I'd also done a couple of films in New York, including *Sea of Love.* John took me around and introduced me to everyone—he basically vouched for me. His actions said "This one's okay, he's one of us." So they let me in the club.

As I left for the day, the script supervisor walked over to me and said, "They liked you upstairs; you'll be back." Well, that one day turned into twenty-some episodes and some of the best work I've ever done. But it was two pieces of luck: A, the fact that I hadn't worked in so long and *had* to take the job, and B, the fact that John Spencer was there and I could relax with a friend. The very thing that I was resisting turned into a remarkable gig and led to some other wonderful things. Of course, there's no question the writing in that show was brilliant, and showing up for one day of *The West Wing* is a little bit different than showing up for one day of something else that's just not worthwhile. The writing was part of the luck in that situation, too.

## THE EGG

When I was starting out, a mentor took me aside and said, "Son, you're gonna be doing this for a long time. There's something you need to know—you need an egg." I said, "A what!?" He said, "I want you to get a shoe box and a bunch of envelopes and bring them to me." So I did. He sat down and on the front of those envelopes, he wrote *rent, education, food, research, advertising,* and *head shot.* And on the last envelope, he wrote *the egg.* He said, "When you get a job, you need to take a piece of that job and put it in the egg to feed it, because there's going to be a period of time when you don't have a job and that egg's going to have to feed you. So I want you to look at all these envelopes in front of it. Those are the ones that have to be taken care of whether you have a job at the moment or not."

### WHAT TO DO WHEN THERE IS NO WORK

- Learn a poem every day.
- Write.
- Study paintings in a museum.
- Go to lunch with someone and, in the middle of it, do an emotional preparation of someone with a sore tooth until your friend says, "Are you all right?"
- Work on a character you'll probably never be cast as.
- Find a Bill Esper or a Larry Moss or a Patsy Rodenburg or an Ellen Geer and trust your instrument to them. I could barely read aloud when I started. I had a lot of help along the way.

For more go to http://www.nowyoutellmebooks.com/actors

I've passed his advice on to a lot of actors, telling them, "We live in a shoe box economy. These are your first responsibilities, but make sure you take care of the egg because the egg's going to have to take care of you." And to this day, I still take a piece of the job and put it away because health insurance comes due or the kids need to go to the doctor, or whatever it is.

I read that the average working actor makes about $40,000 a year; it takes $70,000 for a family of five just to subsist in Los Angeles. So you'd better have another creative way to earn money because $70,000 minus $40,000 is $30,000, and you need to be able to come up with the other $30,000 in a way that doesn't kill you or drain you or demoralize you. Hopefully, you can make it doing something that'll make you laugh a couple of times a day.

But that's just the financial aspect of it. There's also a different kind of wealth. I'm one of the few people I know in my age group, with my background and my education, who can wake up in the morning and think, "I wonder what's going to happen next. I wonder what it'll be." I didn't see *Grey's* coming. I didn't see *The West Wing* coming. There's nothing better than thinking, "Wow, when did this get here?" That's a remarkable way to live.

You need faith that things will be all right; your history says it's going to be all right, and grace says it's going to be all right. Some people call it luck. My first daughter's middle name is Grace because I feel like I've had so much of it. Part of it is that element of something showing up to help you along your path. You can call it a lot of things—the universe, or God—but it's there. We come into the world with it, it may well be coded on our DNA for all I know. But I make sure I'm always appreciative, that I never take it for granted. There are a lot of talented people out there that haven't had the opportunities that I've had, people who can act circles around me. But I showed up. And as far back as I can remember and as far forward as I can see, that's the actor's job. To show up. ★

For more from Michael go to
http://www.nowyoutellmebooks.com/actors.

# CHARLES BUSCH

## "Create an Environment Where Luck Can Find You"

Charles Busch is the author and star of such plays as *The Lady in Question, Red Scare on Sunset,* and *Vampire Lesbians of Sodom,* which ran for five years, becoming one of the longest running plays in off-Broadway history. His play *The Tale of the Allergist's Wife* ran for 777 performances on Broadway and won Mr. Busch the Outer Critics John Gassner Award as well as received a Tony nomination for Best Play.

He wrote and starred in the film versions of his plays *Psycho Beach Party* and *Die Mommie Die,* the latter of which won him the Best Performance Award at the Sundance Film Festival. In 2003, Mr. Busch made his directorial debut with the film *A Very Serious Person.* He is also the subject of the documentary film *The Lady in Question is Charles Busch.*

To this day, he has never gotten a part through auditions.

## IN THE BEGINNING . . .

I always, always wanted to be an actor. I can't remember when I didn't want to be on stage. My father wanted to be an opera singer; he had a lovely voice, but life intervened and he couldn't pursue it. He had a record store in Yonkers, New York, but he kept his hand in doing summer stock and community theater. The first theater I saw was when he took me to the old Metropolitan Opera House to see the great soprano Joan Sutherland perform. That was my first experience with a live performance, and it very much informed my esthetic—which is very 19th century romantic.

My mother's older sister, Aunt Lillian, lived in Manhattan, and I would spend weekends with her. She lived in Murray Hill at Park and Thirty-seventh. My mother died when I was seven. When I was thirteen, I moved into Manhattan with Aunt Lillian. By then she was a widow, and she adopted me. Ever since then I've lived in New York.

Aunt Lillian had started taking me to Broadway shows when I was eight years old. I was never very good as an actor in the traditional sense, but I longed to be out there on that stage.

Truthfully, I think I loved it too much. Some of the other kids with a much simpler relationship to performing—they were confident and they didn't really care that much, thinking, "Oh, it's fun to be in a school play"—were better. I was so gaga about being on stage that I couldn't remember a line. I was stage struck and cautious at the same time, just breathing in the perfume of the theater.

Aunt Lillian was wonderful; any interest I had, she cultivated. I was taking acting classes from age eleven or twelve on, and she sent me to some esoteric summer camp for "sensitive" children that was all theater and art. As a kid I wasn't thinking about a grown-up career. I didn't think past the moment, which meant wanting to be a child star. I sent my picture in when they were casting the movie *Oliver!*. I wrote my first play when I was about eleven. I just wanted to be an actor somehow.

In many ways, it's a curse to be stage-struck. It really is. I think of brilliant people I know, and say, "If they could've just used their brain power in a different direction, that girl could be the editor of *Vogue*." Or, "that man could be president of a corporation." But no, they'd rather be broke and be in the theater.

## COLLEGE

When I was going to go to college, my aunt insisted that I get a liberal arts education. When I applied to schools, it was always to be a theater major. I didn't get accepted to any of the schools I auditioned for. Then I got into Northwestern University, which is a good school. To this day, I don't know what they were thinking. My grades were very mediocre, as were my SAT scores. However, there was no audition required. Northwestern once had a very famous acting teacher, Alvina Krause, who was legendary. Her students were famous people whom you'd read about like Charleton Heston, but by the time I got there, she was long gone and the theater department was in a pretty dead period. After I left they built a huge new complex, and now it's a very good theater program. I probably would've functioned much better if it had been like it is now when I was there. I never liked one minute of school ever; all my life I was so un-academic and so bored. I never functioned well in a classroom situation, but I thought, "Oh, well, at Northwestern, I'll

**Maybe I was too gay or too thin or too whatever it was, but I wasn't right for any part. Ever.**

try again." But I never got the chance. I was never cast in a university play. Maybe I was too gay or too thin or too whatever it was, but I wasn't right for any part. Ever. In those days there weren't any plays with gay characters at all, so I wasn't going to be cast.

## THE GOLDEN AGE OF EXPERIMENTAL THEATER

In the nineteen seventies, the theater landscape in New York began changing. When I came home on vacation, I started seeing experimental theater.

Between 1972 and 1976, it seemed like a whole new landscape: There were plays with naked people! With gritty language! With plots that weren't linear! With plays that were funny and absurd. It was a golden age of experimental theater, with people such as Jess Wise and Charles Ludlam.

When I first saw Charles Ludlam doing a play called *Eunuchs of the Forbidden City*, this outrageous Chinese melodrama, I was dazzled. It was like I'd just had water thrown on me. For the first time, I saw a brilliant writer/actor/director who had all the same interests as me, a love of movies like mine, and an androgynous nature. The whole concept of a theater experience being whatever you wanted it to be, completely outside the genre constraints of Broadway comedies and musicals, infatuated me.

And I thought, "I can write!" I'd begun writing stories to entertain my roommate in college, doing improvs as a woman, and creating my own old movie dialogue. When I saw Ludlam, it all clicked into place. I felt like I could do what he did; in a way, I already was doing it. It was like I'd been handed a magic key and was told, "You can create your own theatrical universe if you so choose." It echoed how I'd been raised by my aunt; there was no sense of "You can't do that," or "What would people think?" Consequently, I didn't have thoughts of, "I can't dress in drag in a play," or, "I can't put on a play in a bar." For me it was like, "Wouldn't it be *fabulous*? Wouldn't it be *great*?"

> **You can create your own theatrical universe if you so choose.**

I was raised in such a protective, safe kind of way that everything seemed so decadent and cool. To this day, if I run into a friend who says they're going to do *My Fair Lady* in some tacky dinner theater, I would say it sounds kind of fun! Some might be kind of embarrassed when they say it, but I would pry. It would sound like an adventure, and anything is worth the anecdote to me. If becoming a good actor comes out of it, it's worth the experience, no matter how awful.

## YOUR OWN JOURNEY

I went back to college for my senior year. I still felt like an outsider. I had terrible stage fright; I just could not participate in the class. I started thinking that there were no roles that I wanted to play, no suitable, famous parts for men (i.e., Blanche Dubois).

Realistically, there were no parts that were suitable for *me*.

I thought, "What do I do?" All I wanted to do was act. So I continued writing parts for myself, purely to entertain friends.

I loved it. I had a real sense of "This is who I am." You're lucky if you're born with a natural sense of who you are, and if not, you've got to figure it out. Your whole career, your life, is a journey into self awareness—and I'm still trying to figure it out. You have to have a big, strong head, full of self-awareness and be very honest with yourself and know what you're selling. You have to sell something that's really who you are. You can't sell a fake product.

It was painful for me, this very young person, to figure out how to do this. There are a lot of people who don't accept whatever their differentness is and continually wonder why they never get cast in standard parts. Fortunately, I realized early on: "That's not going to be me—and I don't want to be that person." I knew that I had an androgynous nature and I could somehow easily channel an old movie actress persona; it just came out naturally.

After I saw Ludlam, I wrote a piece about a traveling freak show in which my best friend Ed and I were these Siamese twin showgirls. At the time, Northwestern had absolutely no venues for self-produced theater, but I knew this guy, a student, who was a real go-getter. He ran a midnight movie theater that showed John Waters' movies and stuff. He lost the rights to a movie one weekend, and he said, "I'll give you the budget I'd use to rent the movie if you want to perform the play." It was really very exciting. They even sent a kid from the campus newspaper to interview me. He was so quiet that he didn't ask me any questions, so I just kept telling him all about the play and everything we were going to do. Then on the day of the performance, on the front page of the Daily Northwestern was this big picture of Ed and me in drag that said, "Degeneracy Reigns at Midnight Madness."

We immediately sold out.

It was really very thrilling and the audience all seemed to go for it. And I knew those kids hadn't seen anything like Charles Ludlam—or me—before.

I idolized Charles Ludlam. His company came to the University of Chicago when I was still at Northwestern, and my friend Ed and I schlepped all the way to the west side to see them. They did a workshop in the afternoon and performed at night.

Afterwards, one of the younger members of the company invited us to come to the cast party back at their hotel. Since it was so late, we ended up being stranded and ended up crashing in their hotel room. It was all very innocent, but what a memory.

After graduation, I wasn't really sure what to do. Should I come home to New York City and start a career? I wasn't completely sure who I was yet, and I'd had this wonderful experience of putting on another play, called *Sister Act,* for a weekend. So I stuck around Chicago for two years.

During those two years I was experimenting. I was in a couple of little plays, not the main part. I started writing my own pieces and putting them on. I started a theater company with a Sartre play of all things. I had a fantasy of creating a local theater company. I wrote a play, a kind of Madame X spoof, and we started performing it all over Chicago in weird venues. Every kind of bar, even some real scary, macho guy beer bars, and here I'm in drag playing a sort of Bette Davis character. It was interesting. We also did midnight shows after movies, and we played in gay clubs.

**I realized I could hook in an audience. That gave me confidence to think I was on the right track.**

It was all very important in my development; I was getting my own sense of power in performing, even in this rough stage. I realized I could hook in an audience. That gave me confidence to think I was on the right track. I had a lot of drive.

Leaving Chicago was bittersweet. From the beginning, I'd told the theater group what kind of company I wanted, and I'd made it clear I was the star. They suddenly didn't want that, and it went very badly. That was the nudge I needed to come back home to New York.

## PAYING IT FORWARD

Back in New York, I jumped in. I decided I would be the writer and the performer and not need to depend on anyone else. In that spirit, I put together a one-man show. But it was one night here, two nights there.

I desperately wanted Charles Ludlam to see me perform to see how talented I was. I almost stalked him, and he finally came to see my act, my cabaret. Afterwards, he set it up so that I could do my show late-night on weekends at his theater. It was a lovely break for me. This gave me a chance to be somewhere long enough that, if an audience liked me, they could go and tell their friends. I was playing for gay crowds for the first time. I started getting my name out as an advocate in the gay paper, and they supported me and were doing stories on me.

It also gave me a chance to be in one of Charles's plays for a little while. That was what I needed to do to get it out of my system. I realized I didn't want to be in Ludlam's company: I wanted to be the star.

A side note: Years later, when we were doing *Vampire Lesbians* off-Broadway, an actor named John Epperson wrote me a fan letter and invited me to see his play. I went and saw it, and it was fabulous. And I said to my director, Kenneth Elliot, "He's great. We need to do for him what Ludlam did for me and produce him at our theater for a late show." That became a really good break for John. He got a lot of attention and it got him on his way.

## GETTING STARTED

Some things change, but one holds true: the important thing is the people you know, your peers, who are going to help you if you are talented and driven.

I was lucky that in the late seventies, the East Village was kind of crazy. It had these little clubs that don't really exist anymore—but even today, *there's always someplace.* If you're not a snob about it, and you don't have highfalutin notions about who you think you are or what you think is right for you, you can put on a play anywhere. Find a bar where you can convince the owner that, since people don't show up until eleven p.m., you can bring people in around eight to see a show and he'll sell more drinks. Convince someone to let you do a play where no one has done a play, and just be up there and perform.

Certainly I've met people who've thought, "Oh, it's beneath me to do that." But I think, "What, you'd rather be an office temp?"

If you want to act, find an opportunity to do it. It'll become harder when you belong to the union. So take advantage when you're just starting out, and put on a play for real cheap—for nothing, if you're clever. But you have to convince people, and you have to keep busy; you can't just sit back and dream and wait for the opportunity. Lots of people have put on plays in strange hovels and it's never gone any further than that, but at least they've put on a show and they're out there. *Nothing can happen to you unless you're out there.*

**You have permission. Go do it.**

Find a young writer or a young director, and offer your services to them, and together you'll discover yourselves. Young struggling playwrights who've never had a play done would welcome your enthusiasm. Find a place where you don't have to pay rent or a bar where you just split the gate. You've got to keep looking and thinking out of the box. You don't need to wait for a "gatekeeper" to say you may pass. You don't need to wait for anyone to give you permission. Or, if you do, here: You have permission. Go do it.

When we first started doing shows in the Limbo Lounge it was literally thirty-five dollars for postage to send out flyers. And then when things got bigger it cost $5K to put on a show, but we would put that on a credit card, and we had an audience already so we'd make our money back.

# MAKING A LIFE

## CHARTING MY OWN COURSE

My goal has always been to earn a living in the theater. When I came back to New York, I was a solo performer. I had a director, but I never had any manager or agent. I booked myself in non-profit theaters around the country. I learned so much about writing and acting and performing for different audiences. I built a reputation in different cities and got to the point where I was getting rave reviews in the *Washington Post, the San Francisco Chronicle*—major papers—and I did very well in the cities.

But I couldn't work enough to earn a living, so between trips, I did every kind of horrible job. If there was a temp job, a receptionist job at a zipper factory, I did it. Or a quick draw sketch artist. Or working for a sports handicapping service, or selling hot typewriter ribbons that fell off a truck, I did it. One day I tried working for a cleaning service. I don't know how to clean an apartment, so the old lady who hired me cleaned the apartment, and I just looked at her scrapbooks with her, and it made her feel good. It was really a terrible thing. Period.

## DOUBTS

As the years went by, I began to have doubts. Some people gave me a hard time saying, "Oh, you're such a late bloomer." Really? At twenty-nine years old, people are picking me out to be the failure? It was scary and very depressing. You begin to wonder, "Is this ever going to happen? When will I know to give up the dream? Is there an expiration date on dreams?"

But whenever I thought for about five minutes, I realized there was nothing else I'd like to do. Nothing. I just assumed it was going to work out, but it was frustrating. I was like Fanny Bryce at the beginning of *Funny Girl*, "That's going to be me up there!" One man I was dating stopped returning my calls because I was obnoxious. We would go see a show and I would sit there and be like, "That ought to be me on stage and my name up on that marquee!" I assumed that if I just kept at it with total blinders on and focused straight ahead, never deviating from that course, kept learning and kept getting better, kept growing, and just kept doing it, that eventually something good was going to happen.

**Is there an expiration date on dreams?**

And yet I really didn't have a specific goal. Or maybe it's that my goals were too realistic. Maybe I would be a bigger star if my goal had been to win the Tony or the Oscar or star in my own sitcom. Instead, I decided I wanted to get my act booked in San Francisco, and I just focused on that and did the act in San Francisco. And it was next goal now met, next goal met.

The farthest my dreaming went was that I wanted to perform my one-man show off Broadway. I thought I could meet somebody who could raise the money, but it never worked out.

Joan Rivers is a good friend of mine. Once when we were talking, I brought up an actress who had a distinguished career but didn't get her first Broadway role until she was eighty. And Joan said, "You never give up! At eighty years old, it could happen."

But as I neared thirty, I didn't think I could go through another ten years of acting and temp work: at forty, still living like that? Thank God I didn't have to face it.

## LUCKY BREAKS

Sometimes I see very talented people and think, "Gee, that wonderful actress! I wonder why she left the business. She was beautiful, a really good comedian, and not neurotic!"

I'd be lying if I didn't admit that a major element of a successful acting career is luck. But *you have to create an environment where luck can find you.* That is really important. You're not going to find luck if you're sitting at home watching reality TV. You have to create the opportunity that will cause your lucky break.

**You're not going to find luck if you're sitting at home watching reality TV.**

Here's how mine finally happened. It was 1984. I was thirty years old and very discouraged because it seemed like I wasn't progressing. I had a circuit of theaters where I'd performed around the country, but it just wasn't going any further. I still wasn't known in New York, for all intents and purposes, and was doing more temp work than performing. It was pretty dismal.

At that point a friend of mine said she was doing an act at an after-hours bar/art gallery in the East Village called the Limbo Lounge. It was a dangerous neighborhood back then: burned-out buildings and crack addicts. But there were also pockets of interesting galleries. I was nervous going there to see her perform. The place was a store front—and it was outrageous. The crowd was gay, straight, punk; I didn't know *what* they were. They had green and pink hair and spoke with fake Bulgarian accents. I was dazzled.

There wasn't a stage. My friend just performed at the end of the room. I was enraptured by the whole decadent atmosphere. It seemed to me like Berlin in the twenties. That night I found this punk kid who was the owner. His name was Michael Limbo. I said, "I have to perform here." He didn't ask me any questions. He said, "I've got an opening three weekends from now." I said, "I'll take it!"

At that point, I was performing alone at a space called the Duplex, and no one was coming anyway. I wanted a change. I wanted to be decadent and outrageous at this place, and I wanted to work with other people. I didn't want to be alone.

I had three weeks to figure out what to do.

Once while working as a temp, I read *Interview with the Vampire* in about a half an hour. I thought, "Okay. I'll be in drag and be this glamorous vampire actress. If I do this right, we can spend zero money."

How do you spend zero money? There was no stage so we didn't need a set. That also meant I had to write a play where everyone was standing up, because there was nowhere to sit down.

In the stories I usually wrote, I had to play all of the characters. So it was fun to write for a (small) cast. My imagination really came alive. We'd have the old movie actress, the countess, the old jazz singer, the old Irish fisherman. I could pick the parts I wanted to play and get others to do the rest.

As for costumes, well, first off, I knew I wanted to be in drag. Then I picked historical periods for which I could get costumes for nothing, with zero money. For example, if it was ancient times, we could just wear a G-string and piece of fabric. My friend Bobby, who was playing one of the centurions, took an old leather jacket and cut it up and stapled it together to make little loin cloths. I wanted to make capes for the succubae to wear, so I took these tacky satin drapes that I had used in a Renaissance faire and we made the capes. Then I went and looked in my aunt's closet. She had this great old dress from the nineteen thirties. I said, "Oh, can I borrow that dress?" I didn't want to tell her the whole story just yet. She asked, "So who's going to wear it? What size is she?" And I said, "About my size."

It was supposed to be just one weekend, and it was just for fun. So who else could I get to do it with me? I started with Ken Elliott, who was my roommate. Like me, he was very discouraged by being thirty years old and trying to be a director when no progress had been made. He had been accepted to Columbia Law School and planned to start in the spring. I told him to just direct me in this last play/skit—what a jazzy way to end his career. So he helped me put it together. Then I went to my friend Andy from the old days at summer camp; at thirty-one he had never been cast in a play. I'd met Theresa when I was in Washington, D.C. and I'd seen her in some play. She was odd and fascinating, so I wrote her in. And Bobby,

I was dating him; he was just so pretty, and I wanted to write him in with his clothes off. For the succubus, I thought of this actress, Lola Pashalinski, who was with Ludlam's company; she was a good twenty years older than we were and a star in the avant-garde.

It was just so much fun, we all hit it all off so well! The rest of the cast didn't know each other, but they all knew me.

I was working as a temp so I thought, "How can I use this?" I drew a flyer by hand, went to the Xerox machine and ran off some copies. We put the flyers up on the street, and sent some out. We spend thirty-six dollars; it was a three cent stamp.

The space could only hold sixty people. We each invited ten people, so we were sold out.

It went so well that weekend that they booked us for another weekend. And then my big dilemma was that, after one weekend, Lola was really over it. She was almost sixty years old; who could blame her? I was desperate to find an actress for the second weekend. I called everybody I knew and it didn't sound terribly appealing to them. I went to this bar in a horribly dangerous neighborhood and I said, "I have this play, *Vampire Lesbians*," and even there, everybody seemed to be busy. Even my own sister wouldn't do it.

My last resort was Julie Halston, this kind of brassy, loud girl I sort of knew from San Francisco. She did a comedy act that was . . . horrible. But she'd come to see my act and said, "You're talented." So at least she had taste. Most important, she said, "I'll do it." I asked, "Have you ever acted before?" She said, "I played Nina in *The Seagull*." And I knew she'd fit right in.

With that we were complete, this ragtag little company. We were each there purely for the fun of it—but "there" happened to be in the right place at the right time. The East Village was just being discovered for its performance art and singing. Things went so well, we decided to do another play called *Theodora, She-Bitch of Byzantium*. I wrote that very quickly. When it came time to perform it, there was a terrible heat wave, which was unexpected in

June. So we ended up doing it outside the venue, in their backyard. *People* magazine came and covered it—we got a big picture in *People*.

Soon we started to get a following. The guys who ran the space decided to move to a larger garage space on Ninth Street where they'd actually have a platform. They invited us to be in residence there; we thought it would be fun. We could do a different play every few weeks.

With that opportunity, we took the performances more seriously. We actually raised five hundred dollars and got some folding chairs and some lights. A number of years before, Ken had started a little summer theater in Indianapolis, and he still had a non-profit status.

I still wasn't thinking of this in terms of a career move; it was more of a detour. But it was fun and exciting, and we all got along so well. It was so sweet.

## FINDING LIKE MINDS

Working with this group was fantastic. The company I'd tried to start in Chicago just hadn't gotten what I was trying to do. They were using the gig as a steppingstone to a "real" career, and therefore thought it was horrible that we were performing in strange, non-theater places.

But this little group in New York was made up of people I'd known from different places. At times I felt like Peter Pan, collecting these lost boys and girls. They were all so thrilled that I'd written a part just for them; they were all just transported by the whole experience. "We're on stage! And we've got makeup on! And people are watching and laughing and cheering." I got really choked up when I thought about it. In my whole life, I'd never really been part of a group. I wasn't really raised in any religion; I was an isolated kind of person. But this little group of people thought I had so much to offer. They loved me and wanted to be part of my fantasy world and play there with me.

## MOVING ON UP

Meanwhile, Ken Elliot, who had spent the last decade trying to be a director, woke up one day to discover he had this whole theater company, somehow by accident. He started to put off going to Columbia Law School which was not a popular decision with his parents, who felt like an evil genius had jumped in and grabbed him. Ken was a very dignified, serious person, and while he had directed, he never produced a show, really. Somehow he figured out how to do it.

At the beginning Ken was the one who got the folding chairs and arranged the lights. We started doing all of these plays and somehow got enormous praise and developed a following. In a matter of months, people were lining up down the block to see this silly piece. It was the most fun ever.

At first we charged three dollars, then five. As soon as the show was over, Ken and I would go back across town to the West Village. We'd eat at this restaurant called McGill's, and we'd have money. Ken said, "Would it be insane if this was actually what we're supposed to be doing? That this is the commercial idea that's eluded us for a decade?"

Ken figured out that we should move to off-Broadway, to a real theater. We were nervous about having to raise money, but it was getting harder to come up with these new pieces to keep the audience coming back.

Ken worked out a deal for a mini-contract; most contracts are designed so that you can't make your money back, but he figured out a budget that added more money. Ours was a small thing, not a Broadway show. We didn't need two million dollars; the original budget was $55K, which is ridiculously low—but to us it seemed enormous.

We raised the money within six months. We just doggedly pursued it. Someone said, "If it's one person, it's a dream; if it's a group, it's a reality." When I was alone, a solo performer, I only had a certain amount of energy I could put out. Now I had Ken and Julie and everybody's energy—and everyone's mother, and everyone's aunt, and all these Jewish widows, putting in their $5K.

At the time I lived in a crummy building. A beautiful apartment but a crummy area. It didn't stop me. I had my sisters and my aunt over for dinner; it wasn't to just have them over but to hit them up for cash. My sister exaggerates that there was just spaghetti and nothing else, but I think there was salad too. I laid it on the line: This is it. This is my moment and if it's ever going to happen, this is it and you've got to cough it up. And they did. Everybody. Ken's parents, even though they thought I was the evil genius, they came through.

For ten years leading up to that time, I was pretty much always broke. And I'm here to tell you, it can be humiliating when you go out and your friends pick up the tab for you and you let them because you need to. You're grateful, but there's still something patronizing about it. On the other hand, there were friends who for many years had said, "If you need anything I'll be there." Then when the time came that I actually did need something, they suddenly backed off. It was interesting to see who came through and who didn't.

I have to say how much I owe to Ken, having the business sense and taking us forward. I couldn't have done it without him. From that time, whenever I have an idea, I'm very lucky that Ken and Carl get going and make it happen.

## WE'RE OPENING!

After all this, one day it hit me: This is actually going to be a real off-Broadway show! It wasn't how I had originally imagined my debut, in a G-string and a wig and high heels, but, hey! It's an off-Broadway show!

We went to rehearsal and had real costumes made.

Shortly before we started previews, I panicked. I thought, "Oh my God, I'm finally going to be reviewed by the major New York newspapers for the first time in my career, in this silly piece that I wrote in a couple of hours! It was just meant to be performed for a weekend in this bar! I did a rewrite to try and make it literary—and just totally wrecked it. I gave Ken the rewrite, and he said he had this terrible nightmare that the audience booed and said, "This isn't the play we want!"

So we went back to the original.

We ended up expanding it to about forty minutes, which still isn't long enough for a show, so we paired it with another piece called *Sleeping Beauty, or Coma*, which we did as the first act.

Opening night was just a magical thing. Sure enough the *Times* came; all the critics came. After we finished the performance, all our friends were being rushed down to the green room. Everybody was on an opening night high. And this sort of homeless kid, Joey, was working back stage pulling the curtain. He ran out to the newsstand and came back in and said, "The *Times* is out!" I was shaking so hard I couldn't read it, and Ken couldn't read it. And so Joey read it out loud, and it was just a rave, rave review. And almost everybody was mentioned in the review. Andy, who'd never been cast in anything, actually had a whole paragraph. Theresa, as well. I went to my dressing room and just wept. I knew it might've not worked out that well. I felt that I had finally risen and that now I was in.

## MAINTAIN THE JOY

The show ran for five years. It became one of the longest running non-musicals off-Broadway; we eventually replaced everybody in the cast, it ran so long. Suddenly, I had a career. I was signed by William Morris. I wrote TV pilots and I could earn a living as a writer. We started our own company, did *Psycho Beach Party*, *The Lady In Question*, and *Red Scare on Sunset*. I wrote plays I wasn't even in, such as *The Allergist's Wife*, which ran on Broadway.

It all came from putting together this little company and doing something fun in the trashiest places. But it wasn't just that. There are other people I know who went all out and were also doing wacky and wild things, and they never moved on. What I learned is, if you're going to do it, be serious about it. Include somebody who has a brain. Think about how you're going to do it. Figure out how to get seats and how to fill them.

So while the decade leading up to this was very difficult, there are advantages to being a ten-year-in-the-making overnight success.

When the New York papers and the theater establishment "discovered me" for the first time, they were seeing someone who'd been going around the country for a decade, building a relationship with the audience. My audiences were my costars for all those years. I knew how to work them and I knew how to share with them. I'd paid my dues, and I'd found my own tribe of actors who brought positive energy we all shared. I had Ken, the business brain.

So when luck came, I was ready.

To any young theater artists, I'd say: Keep learning. Get better. Figure out who you are rather than simply trying to fit into the mold. Get other people involved in your dream. Your peers are struggling as well; maybe together you can figure out a way in.

Most importantly, try to maintain the joy. It sounds sappy and yet, when you start becoming grim in your pursuit, take a step back and remember your passion. That can lead to good things. The audience will respond to your joy. ★

For more from Charles go to
http://www.nowyoutellmebooks.com/actors.

# JULIA MOTYKA

## "Be prepared to feel freaked out."

**J**ulia Motyka is a "triple-threat," who has performed, taught and produced throughout the United States. A veteran Shakespearean actress, she's played Helena in *All's Well that Ends Well*, Juliet in *Romeo and Juliet* and Silvia in *Two Gentlemen of Verona*. She has also appeared in numerous Off-Broadway productions such as *We Got Issues*, produced by Eve Ensler and Jane Fonda, and *The Golden Ladder*. Julia recently played Rachel in a regional production of Craig Lucas' comedy *Reckless,* a role which won her a Westword Best of Denver Award for Best Actress in 2011. Her film work includes *The Kindergarten Shuffle* and the indie film *In the Family*.

Julia has created educational programs for young actors, including the Living Shakespeare program based in New York's Hudson Valley. Julia began her career as a producer at just nineteen, and later co-founded Red Griffin Media, which was involved in the Off-Broadway production of *ROOMS*.

A dyed-in-the-wool New Yorker, she rolls out the welcome mat and offers very practical advice for those who arrive in New York ready to hit the ground running.

# MAKING A LIVING

## WELCOME TO NEW YORK

When you arrive in New York, suitcase in hand, ready to launch your professional career as an actor, there is a relatively standard step-by-step process of what you should do.

**STEP ONE: Get Settled.** The first and most important thing, and the thing most people don't do, is get yourself settled. Factor in six weeks to find an apartment, find a day job—however menial or depressing it may be—find a way to establish a rhythm in your life. Because it's stressful to find an agent. It's stressful to go on auditions. It's a full-time job to establish yourself in that part of the world. Have two months' worth of rent money while you find your job, find your apartment, your deli, your grocery store. Make yourself a home.

**STEP TWO: Head Shots.** Next, you need to get a really good professional head shot. Because before you walk into a room, before your talent comes into play, it is *the* thing that people see. They don't always look at the résumé; they look at your face. And from that picture, they decide whether or not they want to meet you. So . . .

Go to a place called Reproductions at 70 West Fortieth Street (in L.A. they're at 3499 Cahuenga Boulevard West, www.Reproductions.com). They have a huge hardbound book of photographers. You can sit there for free for hours and hours. And you pore over the book.

When you're looking for head shot photographers, look at the eyes of the people in the pictures. Are all of the eyes in the pictures different, or is the photographer taking the same picture of everybody over and over again? Do you see uniqueness in everyone? If the answer is yes—you see six pictures by the same photographer and they all look different but they all look good—that's a person who's really listening to their camera when they capture you. Write down their phone numbers.

Then, go home and call them. If they're good at what they do, they will offer to meet with you over a cup of coffee. Do that! Meet them. Sit down for half an hour. Do you like him or her? Do you get along? Do you feel comfortable? You'll know almost immediately that that's how you feel. If that's the case, ask what they charge. A good head shot photographer, right now, will charge anywhere from eight hundred to fifteen hundred dollars. Some will charge less, but not many; and if they're charging a lot less, look at them very closely. Because they can afford to charge more if they're very good at what they do. Also, if you're a woman, there will be an additional charge for doing your makeup. Get that price up front as well.

Once you've found someone, schedule your time. The shoot will usually take between three and five hours. You'll wear multiple outfits and hairstyles. You can go through as many looks as you like. As an actor, it's important to think about what you want to present as. A young mom? A business woman? A college student? Who can people see you as? Be ready so that when you get in front of the camera, you know what your goals are.

**STEP THREE: Send and Meet.** Next, there are several publications you should get. One is *Backstage,* a vaguely depressing newspaper that lists a lot of open calls and showcases and workshops. Then there are organizations that have popped up over the last ten to fifteen years where you pay small fees to go in and audition and meet with people. They sound like scams, but many of them are not (although you always have to be careful who you go and see; make sure they're reputable). I recommend The Network and One on One (www.thenetworknyc.com/ or www.thenetworkstudioeast .com/new_york_intensives.php or www.oneononenyc.com/), which is really excellent and where you can meet very good agents and quite top-of-the-line casting directors from places such as the Roundabout and Lincoln Center. Really terrific people. A lot of the network television folks come. They also do seminars where you go in and have the opportunity to do your thing and show your wares. If they like you, they keep you on file. And they call you with appropriate opportunities.

Begin to develop not only a community of industry people who are getting to know you, but, at the same time, develop a group of actors who are beginning to get to know you. Find a community of people who are in the same place as you, who are just starting out. So many opportunities, so many good things come out of the Vulcan mind-meld of a group of kids who are just getting started.

> So many good things come out of the Vulcan mind-meld of a group of kids who are just getting started.

From there, chances are, things will start to happen. One person will give you a call to do a workshop or a reading or whatever it is, and you invite the other people that you know. And that list will continue to grow. And eventually, over time, an agent will pick you up. Just keep working!

**IF NECESSARY (BUT ONLY IF NECESSARY): Mailings.** If those things are still struggles after you've gone to lots of meetings and done all of your semipaid networking, and it's still not happening, you can do a more traditional approach, which is an agent mailing. It's not a first-choice route because it's costly and you don't get face time. But if you're really having trouble, you can pick up a book of address labels of all of the franchised agents in Manhattan, and you put together a mailing. The labels are around twenty dollars at the Drama Book Shop (250 West Fortieth Street, www.dramabookshop.com). Then put together a picture and a résumé and a personalized cover letter. To every single person. Do your research. Who do they represent? How long have they been in the industry? Do they do something that you like? So that when you send a letter, it's not "Hi, I just got off the bus from Toledo," but "Hi, this is what I'm working on. I know you represent X. I really admire her career and how you've handled that. I'd love to be seen by you. Thanks."

Then keep following up every six weeks. Send a postcard, send a little note. Invite them to something. Because people remember who's in front of them.

## THE FIRST EIGHT MONTHS

We're communal beings. However introspective or however solitary we are, we all thrive on contact: emotional, physical contact with people. That's why you must find a community of mentors or friends, or even just your classmates in a yoga or exercise class. It's especially important to be around people when you're new in town; it will give you a sense that New York is a village as opposed to a metropolis or, worse, an isolating wasteland.

There does seem to be an eight-month window when people arrive in New York during which it is really hard. Everybody I know who comes experiences it; and, astonishingly, it always lasts about eight months. You get here, and the first few weeks are fabulous and amazing, and then . . . you have no friends. Or you have some friends, but they have lives. They're really busy. It's not usual in Manhattan to see a friend once a month. Nobody's got the time. And so you're lonely. And you don't have acting jobs yet; you don't have an agent. You don't know what you're doing yet. You get scared. And it takes eight months to slowly begin to feel like you have a routine, you know the ropes, you feel successful. You have friends who you can see on the weekend; you have people who call you, people you can call. You have a teacher or two whom you really like and admire, who you can go to for advice. You either have an agent or you know how you're going about getting one. And that's when your life starts to begin like it belongs to you again.

But for that first eight months, just kiss it good-bye. Be prepared to feel freaked out a lot of the time. And lonely a lot of the time. Maybe in knowing that, it will help. It goes by.

## MAKE A BUDGET

From the beginning, it's important to put yourself on a realistic budget. It's all well and good to say you'll live on twenty-two dollars and eat tuna fish every week. You can't. I had catsup sandwiches for several days in a row one year and it's really no fun. You can't do it. So, even though you're broke (or especially when you're broke), create a realistic budget that takes into consideration what you really need. You will not walk seventy blocks to an audition in January, so don't pretend that you will. I used to get into this mentality of "I'm really broke so if I spend even less than I think I can . . ." You can't. You will just overspend and then be miserable.

> **It's all well and good to say you'll live on twenty-two dollars and eat tuna fish every week. You can't.**

When you don't have a lot of money, it's about being creative and being thrifty. Cook at home. Be the geek who brings her lunch. Do the things that save you money (even if you have money, frankly). I pack a lunch when I'm doing a theater job all the time. Learn to economize a little bit so if it takes three or four months instead of the two you were expecting to get another job, you're not destitute.

If it takes six months—and sometimes it will—keep your day jobs active. Don't go back to them if you don't have to, but keep those relationships warm, so that if, God forbid, there's a really slow year, you've got something to fall back on. A friend of mine is a fabulous actor, works all the time, and still had fourteen months when he couldn't get shot in an alley. Another friend who worked all the time, had a catering job and thought he would never have to go back, but last year, he did. Every now and then, it gets that slow. It doesn't mean you've lost your talent and you'll never work again, though it feels like it at the time. But it is good to have a couple of options. And that is frankly a moment where having other interests is helpful. If you stay in the business long enough, there will be a year where you don't work—and six months of that year where you have two auditions and you really want to tear your hair out—so having other things you love to do comes in handy. Try to find a way you can make money doing something that's fun and creative for you so you're not going back to a waitressing job or a secretarial pool; you're going back into an area of your life that you really enjoy and can make a little money.

For me, it's always been education. I do have a fair amount of classical theater in my background, and often when you do Shakespeare in regional jobs, there's often an educational component, where they send working artists into schools to teach. I found it's something that I really enjoy. I really enjoy the lightbulb moment of the little kids figuring it out—understanding the classical text. I just think it's the cat's pajamas. So for me, I came home from a job four years ago, and I didn't have very much money in my bank account, and I really wasn't sure what the next job was. So through friends, I started a Shakespeare program for little kids in Westchester. It was one day a week, on weekends, so I could go on my auditions. It was not a great living, but it was enough money to keep me safe between jobs. And I really, really liked it! I still do it whenever I have ten weeks when I know I'm not going anywhere. Things like that are really terrific. If you get creative with the things you enjoy, you can come up with some remarkable ways of making some extra money.

A friend of mine started a business about becoming a working actor because she was having such a hard time. It's all about marketing yourself as an actor. Why not? It's what she was becoming an expert in at the time!

Everybody who goes into this is creative. Think about the things you do. Chances are there's some money in there somewhere. Finding ways of being proactive, finding ways of empowering yourself, is really important.

## WALKING INTO AN AUDITION

When I first started, I thought the most important thing about an audition was walking into a room and being fabulous, or being the character, or being some idea of something. What I've come to realize is that auditioning is really the art of learning who you are, with great specificity, so that when you walk into the room, you are exactly yourself. You're the same and best self that you'd be if you were with a best friend, or a parent, or someone you felt incredibly close to. Because the thing we try to share when we do our work is that sense of intimacy. That sense of you know me, and I know you, and we're going to fall in love together around this play.

That means you want to walk into an audition and are at ease in your own skin, and with the material. Initially, it was really hard for me to remember that the people on the other side of the table are just people. They're colleagues, and they're there working, just like you. And so to assume a certain level of camaraderie.

> **Auditioning is really the art of learning who you are, with great specificity, so that when you walk into the room, you are exactly yourself.**

## AUDITIONS: THE PILLOW TALK

I have the great benefit—and I guess, sometimes, curse—of being married to a director. It's really interesting to hear him talk about casting. Before any actor even walks into the room, we'll talk the night before auditions: "I'm really looking for this type of actor, and I really see the character like this"; a very specific list of things he's looking to fulfill.

When you have an agent, and you're called in for an audition, you know you're of a type that they're looking for. I'm tall and blond. Generally, I sit in rooms with tall blond women. But within that, how tall? How blond? How thin? How blue-eyed? How green-eyed? How this, how that? What strengths do you possess as an actress? Where do you fit within the type that they're looking for? It is a matter of talent, yes. But it's talent plus the specificity of slotting into the idea that people have of what they want.

And that's something that's very hard to get used to. Because you're used to going into an audition and thinking, "Well, I'll be brilliant. And it doesn't matter that they want a fifty-five-year-old African American; I'm fabulous! Who cares that I'm blonde and twenty-seven? Who cares?" It doesn't really work that way 99 percent of the time. Of course, every now and then there are those times when the perception of the people behind the desk does get changed by what you do; the director wanted someone who's six foot two with big bushy black hair, and someone who's five feet and bald gets the job. So, while the truth is they're looking for specific things, that shouldn't stop anybody from going in and being fabulous and doing as much as possible to change someone's mind.

## THE SUCCESSFUL AUDITION

I have left auditions feeling miserable and like I've tanked, and then gotten a callback. Sometimes I've left auditions feeling like I was brilliant and a genius, and never heard another peep. Sometimes I've felt I was brilliant and then gotten terrible feedback. So you never really know. A successful audition is an extension of what I was just talking about. Being able to go in, trust yourself, be all of yourself, and trust that if that's who they're looking for, that's enough. You do your work, you enjoy it, you have your moments of truth, your moments of comedy—whatever it is you're looking for in that given piece—and leave and let it go.

For me, the most successful auditions are the ones where I am excited but calm walking into the room and peaceful walking out of the room. I did my piece, I showed up, I did my work today. Now I'm going to go home or go on to the next one, and whatever will be will be.

The time it gets tricky—and we all do this—is when you go into the room and do your stuff and leave, and you find yourself thinking about it six hours later. And twelve hour later. And, "Oh, I really want that one! It would be so great and I'm so right for it, and I was so wonderful . . ." But it isn't really up to you. There's a line between wanting a part in a healthy and good way, and wanting it so much that you keep yourself up at night and are heartbroken when it doesn't come along.

I wish there was a way actors could be taught how to let it go. How to walk in and do your best and offer yourself in all of your vulnerability and all of your you-ness, and then walk out of the room and trust that you're fabulous and you're wonderful and you're going to do brilliant things, even if it's not this brilliant thing.

My dad was a voice teacher and an opera director. When I was sixteen, he said something really wonderful to me. "You know, darling, imagine that you are a Tiffany vase. You're one of a kind. Someone has put you together with the most extraordinary care. You're uniquely beautiful. But you are blue. You are a blue vase. And if you are put on display and somebody wants an orange vase, there is nothing you can do. You are who you are. And the more you know that, the less personally you will take it when someone chooses something else."

While it can make a person feel a little like a commodity, there's a truth in it: that the more confident and comfortable you can be in your own skin, the easier it gets to let go of what someone else wants or doesn't want. That takes a lot of time and a lot of conscious energy. Because what we do is so vulnerable and intimate and immediate, it's a practice to learn how not to take it personally. Like when somebody sort of looks at you and goes, "Well, you're so tall" or, "Maybe if you were different somehow—if something about you was different." But I wish there was some sort of aphorism that you could be handed to learn it. But the thing to know going in is that you will hear, "No." You will not get every job, but that does not mean you're not gifted; it doesn't mean you won't work. It doesn't mean bad things will befall you or that you should have become a firefighter. It just means that this was not the right job.

> **You will not get every job, but that does not mean you're not gifted; it doesn't mean bad things will befall you or that you should have become a firefighter. It just means that this was not the right job.**

## CHOOSE YOUR LEVEL

When you're starting out, it's easy to feel that agents, casting people, and even directors, are so powerful that you need to put yourself in a disempowered position and ask for a job. The sooner you can forget that and think of those people as colleagues—you work *with* your agent, you don't work *for* her; you work *with* a director—the better off you'll be. It seems as though the paradigm is set up so the producer is at the tippy-top, then directors are next in line, and then these people and those people, saving room for the actors at the very bottom of that power structure. It's not that way. Your life will get infinitely easier and more successful and happier the moment you go, "Oh! My agents are my colleagues. They're working from their end, I'm working from my end, and we have the same goals, and we work together. We have a contract together." Finding that balance, particularly as a woman, is very important. It's really easy to think of yourself as "less than," or in a position where you have to cross your fingers and plead or beg. You're not in that position.

Creative people tend to be people-pleasers. We want it so much that it can turn into, "Tell me who I need to be. Tell me what I need to do. Anything. I'll do anything." Interestingly enough, the more you say, "This is who I am, this is what I do. Nice to meet you. Let's work together," (a) you'll find that power feels really good; (b) suddenly the jobs come more frequently and; (c) in a way, they matter less. That's a really important balance to find.

## WORKING RELATIONSHIPS

There's nothing better than acting with a great actor. It's like having really great food, or really great sex. *Yes! Fantastic!* Being with a good actor on stage is like being in perpetual motion. You're always falling, but

---

**JULIA'S STEP-BY-STEP PROCESS FOR LAUNCHING YOUR PROFESSIONAL CAREER**

- **STEP ONE:** Get Settled—Find your job, apartment, local deli, grocery store, etc.
- **STEP TWO:** Head Shots—Reproductions at 70 West 40th Street. (In L.A. they're at 3499 Cahuenga Boulevard West. Website: http://www.Reproductions.com.
- **STEP THREE:** Send and Meet—I recommend The Network (https://www.thenetworknyc.com/ or http://www.thenetworkstudioeast.com/new_york_intensives.php) or One on One (http://www.oneononenyc.com/).
- **STEP FOUR (ONLY IF NECESSARY):** Mailings—Get labels from the Drama Book Shop at 250 W. 40th Street (http://www.dramabookshop.com).

For more go to http://www.nowyoutellmebooks.com/actors

you're always falling together. You know those moments when you're a little kid playing with your best friend? You look across and you lock eyes, and you know you're in the same game, and you're both having the *best time* and it's *the most fun you've ever had*, and it's *scary* and it's also *wonderful*. And you trust them. With your life, you trust them. That's what it's like being onstage with a really great actor. You're just there, playing the best game.

> **Acting with a great actor is like having really great food or really great sex.**

On the other hand, there are different ways actors can be difficult. An actor can be difficult by being late, by not really being present in rehearsal, by not being giving. An actor can also be difficult by getting an idea of what's supposed to be happening in a scene and then just kind of not looking at you and not paying attention to what you are actually doing in real life flesh at that moment. But you can only control what you can control. Do your job. Stay present. Stay active. Be kind. And find one person, whether it's in the cast or outside of the cast in your personal life, who you can vent to without fear of retribution, someone you really trust. Because it's important to be able to come home and say, "This sucked. I hated my job today." And it's equally as important to get up the next day and go back with joy.

The worst problem with a difficult actor is not necessarily that they are difficult, but that they are infectious. So finding a way to safeguard yourself from the infection of boredom or bitchiness or tardiness or laziness is really, *really* important.

Some of the best shows can have a really difficult actor in the lead role. There are people who work all the time who are not easy to get along with. There are actors who have become really successful and consequently really difficult to get along with. You will encounter them. Just do your job.

How I work with a difficult director, however, has changed over time. A difficult director used to completely shut me down, and it was very hard.

I'd go home feeling bereft and bamboozled and like I had eight left feet, because I was always wrong. Not to mention that a difficult director can make a good play not as good. He or she has that kind of power.

One skill you need to develop as an actor is to become director-proof, to hear what a director is saying and learn how to translate it into language that is applicable as an actor. So if you're working with a director who tells you exactly how many steps to take, with what foot, on what line, exactly where to go and how to do it, then, okay. Think of him as a choreographer. And fine, he can fill in the physical life, but now you do the interior. And if that's what he or she wants you to do, do it. There are things that person hasn't dictated to you—that's where your creativity lives.

Conversely, if you're with someone who is giving you line readings, or tells you exactly what emotive quality he wishes to see, don't panic. Say, "Yes, yes, thank you, good. I appreciate that, that's a very good note." And then, frankly, tell them to go buzz off in your head, and go do your work. Because if you're able to do that, then go in and do what you know you're supposed to do to make it wonderful, and authentic, that director will come to you afterwards, without fail, and say, "You see? You did exactly what I told you and it was brilliant!" Meanwhile, in your brain, you're knowing what an ass he is. But on your face, a smile and you say, "Oh, thank you, that was so helpful! It was just wonderful for me, too." You become a yes-man of sorts. Doing what he demands, but leaving space for yourself as well.

# MAKING A LIFE

## OTHER PARTS OF YOUR LIFE

Try to get to a space within yourself where not only do you know who you are and what you do, but where you have other parts of your life to go home to, where there are other parts of your world that you place value in and that place value in you. If I don't get a job and I'm upset about it or frustrated or feel like, "They missed the boat because I was perfect!" then I can come home and can work on the Shakespeare Program for Kids that I've started, or be with a friend, or be with my partner. Or be in the world in a different way that is gratifying, too, that helps feed the moments when the other stuff is slower or heartbreaking.

Find as many things as possible that are satisfying to you. One of the tricks of being a great performer is being a well-rounded person: knowing about the world, knowing who you are and how you exist in that world. So it's a common mistake as a young actor to think "If I don't eat, sleep, and breathe this all the time, I will never be successful." Actually, you can eat, breathe, and sleep it a lot of the time. But fill in with other things, too.

> **One of the tricks of being a great performer is being a well-rounded person.**

There isn't a person alive who doesn't have multiple interests, whether it's horseback riding or knitting or education, dog training, whatever. Find something that you enjoy, that fulfills a different part of who you are. Take pleasure and pride in that, too, so that you're not defined only by one thing.

## EVALUATE

This is something that my husband, Scott, learned from his father, Stephen Schwartz, who's a composer, and quite an astonishing one. When Scott was finishing college, he said, "Give yourself a period of time: a long one, three years, five years, ten years, whatever you feel is necessary. Say, 'I'm doing this [to establish a career in the arts], for this period of time. I'm not going to worry about how I'm doing, where I'm getting to, where I'm not getting to. Just keep going.'"

When you get to the end of that period of time, look back over that course of years and ask, "What have I accomplished? Where am I? Where did I think I'd be? Where did I want to be? Am I on a path that is giving me success, or am I just standing still? Have I hit a wall in some way?"

If you've gotten to a place where things have started to feel possible, say, "Okay!" Then give yourself another period of time. Or maybe you don't need another period of time. Maybe you're ready to say, "I'm doing this for the rest of my life."

But when you get to the evaluation point, if you look around and think, "I haven't been able to work the way I want to, and I want other things in my life, too. I want a family. I want a house, I want to live somewhere else. I want financial stability, I want more flexibility." Whatever it is that you want that you're not getting from your work, if those things start to feel heavier on the balance of your life, listen to that. Because if you don't, it will make you bitter. Staying somewhere when you're resentful of what it's not giving you will not bring good things into your life. So I think that's probably the moment to really consider what else there might be for you. Chances are, it'll be a something good. ★

For more from Julia go to
http://www.nowyoutellmebooks.com/actors.

# BRIAN STOKES MITCHELL

## "Celebrate Being Human"

Dubbed "the Last Leading Man" by the *New York Times*, Brian Stokes Mitchell has enjoyed a rich and varied career on Broadway, television, and film, along with appearances in the great American concert halls. His Broadway career includes Don Quixote in *Man of La Mancha* (Tony nomination and Helen Hayes Award); Fred Graham/Petruchio in *Kiss Me Kate* (Tony, Drama Desk, and Outer Critics Circle Awards); Coalhouse Walker Jr. in *Ragtime* (Tony nomination); as well as August Wilson's *King Hedley II* (Tony nomination); *Kiss of the Spider Woman*; *Jelly's Last Jam*; David Merrick's *Oh, Kay!* and *Mail*, which earned him a Theater World Award for outstanding Broadway debut. His most recent shows were *Women on the Verge of a Nervous Breakdown* on Broadway, and the film *Jumping the Broom*.

# MAKING A LIVING

## AUDITIONS

When you walk into an audition, the most important thing to know is that the people sitting behind the table are not your enemies or adversaries. As a matter of fact, they are *dying* for you to be the right person for the role. It makes their job easier and makes them look good—casting director, director, choreographer—everyone.

## WORKING WITH DIRECTORS

I have found that the most difficult directors are not those at the top or at the bottom of their craft, but those in the middle. The same is true for actors. The bottom ones (in small community theaters, for example) are so happy to be working, and those at the top are confident in their abilities. However, as with anything, there are grand exceptions on both ends of the scale. If the director is incompetent, I just nod my head and say, "Yes" to their advice, then do my own thing when it comes down to the performance. Of course my preference is to work in concert with a director and find the ways we can trust each other and be mutually supportive. I have had the good fortune to work with great directors for most of my career. How do you work with good directors? Listen and learn and trust.

> The most difficult directors are not those at the top or at the bottom of their craft, but those in the middle.

> Fear kills comedy (and tragedy, too, for that matter).

## THE BEST ACTORS

The best actors have taught me how to listen. How to prepare. How to *react*. How to treat others around you with kindness and respect. And to continually work on your craft and yourself.

On the other hand, there's a lot you can learn from bad actors as well! For example, the deleterious effect of selfishness and not being prepared. That fear kills comedy (and tragedy, too, for that matter). Of course, you'd rather not learn such things while on stage.

## YOUR CRAFT

Acting is a living art that changes and deepens as you change and deepen. Never stop learning. Never lose your curiosity or your love of life.

> **Acting is a living art that changes and deepens as you change and deepen.**

Stay in class, certainly, and study—but also read, go to museums, allow everything to inspire and fill you up. Be open to life and to new experiences and to new people and to change.

## SHORT AND LONG FORM ARTS

When it comes to moving between film, television, and stage, my motto is: "Go where I am wanted." The more you can do, the more you work. Each medium has different subtleties in technique, although the basic technique remains the same: finding the truth in your character. I call television and film "short form arts" that favor those who are spontaneous and good at improvisation. Stage is a "long form art" that favors those who are good at delving into the nooks and crannies of a piece and character over (hopefully) a long amount of time. In fact, when you're in a long theatrical run, doing the same part again and again, keep exploring the nooks and crannies of the role. I like to say that art is in the spaces. A great artist continually explores those spaces.

And yet, no matter which form you're working in, the mind-set is the same—to do the best work you can at the time.

## HABITS OF THE SUCCESSFUL ACTOR

While I truly believe that the difference between a talented actor who makes it and one who doesn't is luck, lucky actors, by and large, tend to be those who constantly work on their craft, trying to find new ways to explore their art. Tenaciousness helps. Big time.

**Tenaciousness helps. Big time.**

## WHEN IS IT TIME TO PURSUE SOMETHING ELSE?

Give up acting as a career when you become bitter and frustrated and find yourself hating life and your career and yourself. I am a firm believer that it is a good idea to rewrite yourself every now and then.

# MAKING A LIFE

## MANAGING MONEY

It's easy to manage your money when you have none! What is hard is when you have some. Never spend more than you have: if you can't pay off your credit card completely every month, you are spending beyond your means and getting yourself into debt. As you make more, you can spend more.

My second rule is to be sure you always have some "F.U." money set aside so you don't have to take jobs you don't want!

## WHICH JOBS TO TAKE

I have turned down a lot of jobs that I didn't think were going to lead me to where I wanted to go. I've never done soap operas, for instance. At one time I was offered more money than I had ever made to be on a soap. But, personally, I don't like them; consequently, I would have been very unhappy doing it. I also noted that soaps can be hard to break out of once you get on them or become pegged as a soap actor. That said, soap actors are some of the hardest working actors in show business. There are some very good ones, so this is no slam to them, just a personal choice.

I also would not want to portray someone who was insulting to a race or group of people without the piece having a greater purpose or working for a greater good.

There are also personal and family consequences to be weighed. Part of choosing the life of an artist means that you can't always do what you want when you want. And sometimes a good career choice can be difficult on one's personal life, and vice versa. Those are decisions that each person must make for him or herself.

In general, the criteria I hold for parts that I accept are: first, is it something in which I can excel? We don't usually get the parts in which we can't excel, anyway, so that is not a big worry. Second, I prefer parts that lift the human spirit or illuminate something about the human condition—if not the individual part, at least the piece as a whole.

I want to celebrate being human—in all our glory and pathos. It is my hope that when I leave this planet I will have done more good than harm. ★

For more from Brian go to
http://www.nowyoutellmebooks.com/actors.

# EDEN SHER

# "When you're young, you naturally go with your instincts."

Eden Sher currently plays eternally optimistic middle child Sue Heck on *The Middle*. Other credits include Gretchen on *Weeds* and Carrie on *Sons and Daughters*. Young Eden got her break when she was picked out of her class at school to offer some funny quotes in a Jay Leno segment, which led to a recurring bit that she and her brother did on the show. Casting directors took note, and commercials led to guest shots that led to failed shows that eventually led to successful ones. Though she's graduated from the realm of "child actor," she has plenty to say about the pros and cons of jumping right into the business without benefit of acting school . . . and the pluses and minuses of having so much parental guidance around.

# MAKING A LIVING

## THE RIGHT STUFF

One thing about acting is that before you jump in to try and try and never give up, you need to honestly assess the matter of natural talent. There has to be something there—some sort of spark that allows you to access that creative part of your brain. If you don't feel that you have that, you have to be very honest with yourself.

It sounds contradictory, because on the one hand, you *have* to compare yourself to others, but at the same time, don't compare yourself to anyone else! You sort of have to compare yourself to everyone in the beginning, just to see whether you have what it takes. And then forget about it immediately.

## ON THE JOB TRAINING

You can learn a lot about acting on the job, especially as a kid. I did. I learned what it was like to have to act in front of the camera. Still, I know a lot of people who started on the stage and who would argue that working on a TV set is not the best way to learn. You have to start by learning how to do a live theatrical performance where you've memorized all your lines and develop a certain method. But when you're young, you naturally go with your instincts.

I did take some classes for child acting because my mom wasn't going to let me do this without it. I was a precocious young kid, so I was smart enough to charm people into hiring me. But she said, "If you're going to really try to do this as a career, even if you don't continue on as an adult, you have to take some sort of classes." She thought she was forcing me, but I was like: "Yeahhh! Let me do theater! Let me take acting classes!"

I learned a lot of the basics you'd learn in classes as an adult, and that helped carry me through. But by learning on the job, certain things have been instilled in me so thoroughly that no class could retrain me. Just basic things, like staying in the moment. Listening to your scene partner. Making eye contact.

I was a kid, and kids have a lot of imagination, so I would think: What would this character do in the morning? What would this person do with her mom? When I was fourteen and doing eleven episodes of this show called *Sons and Daughters* on ABC, I wrote it out in a little journal. Of course I could have learned in a class how to keep a character journal. But at the time it was just instinct.

## THE PSYCHOLOGY OF AUDITIONS

Once I started auditioning, my mom kept trying to tell me, "It's not personal. Nothing's personal. It has nothing to do with you. This is not a reflection of your personality at all. They're not rejecting you because you're not great. They're not picking you because they're looking for another type." And when you're eight, nine, ten, and you're auditioning for commercials, it's easy to say, "Oh yeah, they wanted a different type. It's no big deal." But once I really started working, and I was fourteen, fifteen, sixteen, and getting bigger auditions, not just for commercials and episodics but for movies and pilot roles, it got harder to tell myself that.

Often I found myself going up against the same group of about fifteen girls at auditions. There was a five-week period where I almost got four different roles—but each time it went to the same other girl. I began to think of her as a prettier, cuter, skinnier version of me. I refused to believe that it wasn't personal and not something I was doing. I knew the problem was completely me, I was terrible, I shouldn't be an actor, and I definitely shouldn't compete for anything this girl was going up for—was going to get! I was sure the problem was personal; it absolutely was about me!

The next week, even though I was really depressed, I went out for a big guest-starring role on a show. And that same girl was there at the screen test—but I ended up booking it! The kicker is, I saw her months later, and she said, "Oh, congratulations on that part! The second I saw you there,

I thought, why am I even here? This is so stupid." That was a lightbulb moment for me. I thought, "YOU think that? You booked the last five roles that I wanted so desperately!"

But *everyone* feels unworthy. I idolized this girl, and hearing the same words come out of her mouth was a revelation.

When I go into the audition room, I sometimes forget that those people don't know me. They can't reject *me*, because they haven't gotten to know me on a personal basis. Also, not getting a part doesn't mean they don't like you and don't want to hire you for something else. It just means you didn't get that one job.

That was brought home to me when I sat in on a casting session for a show where I'd already been cast, so I was totally relaxed. They'd asked me to read with people who were auditioning for other parts.

> "This is not what we were looking for, but wasn't that [audition] awesome? Man, I wish we could hire her."

I'd always assumed that when actors left an audition, the casting people would look at each other and say, "Aw, she's so stupid. That was a terrible performance. Oh man, did you see what she did there? Ha ha ha!"

Instead, they were all saying, "This is not what we were looking for, but wasn't that awesome? Man, I wish we could hire her."

Seriously. They said it after almost every person. Sometimes I have to force myself to remember that day after I've left an audition and I go into that zone of thinking, "Oh my God, what a stupid choice. I'm so low."

## HIGH-SECURITY SETS

Wouldn't it be nice if there was a happy ending, where I can say I've definitely gotten over my insecurity? You know, for the most part I have. Even when I'm working, though, sometimes I think that I didn't perfect my acting in a certain scene. I didn't get the most perfect take. A lot of actors don't like to express those thoughts to other people because they never want to have even a moment of seeming not confident. But I'm not going to lie to you! I don't think it weakens my character to admit it. Everyone gets a little insecure. It's the nature of the beast. It's what we do, since as actors, we're there performing for other people, hoping that they enjoy us.

Especially when you're doing comedy. Sometimes it's a crapshoot and you really do have to be confident in what you're doing. You have to know that even if they don't laugh, you committed to it and went for it all the way. Doing comedy on a show where there's no live audience is interesting. You can still gauge off what you hear in video village [where the crew watches the take on video as it's being shot], or how the director and other actors respond to it in rehearsal. It definitely is way different when you're working on a multi-cam, when everything you do is right there in your face.

Feedback is very important. It's an integral part of comedy. In drama, if somebody says, "That was a really effective performance," you're not going to argue and say, "No it wasn't. I didn't hear you sobbing!" But in comedy, saying something is funny and just naturally having the reaction of laughter are two different things.

In television, especially after doing it take after take after take, sometimes you really won't get a laugh, just because you've done it five times and they know what's coming. But if someone says, "That was your best take, that was so hilarious," even though you didn't hear uproarious laughter, you have to believe and trust that it's okay.

## AGENTS AND MANAGERS

I didn't have a manager until very recently. I'd say agents are much more important. In my experience, once you've been working, managers have the connections to get you into higher-status meetings, or better auditions, or lots of generals—that is, general meetings with directors, or casting directors of networks, or heads of networks. But you're going to have to go to all those dumb cattle calls for commercials, and an agent does that. So as far as starting out in the business, I'd say absolutely get an agent first. Did you know that anyone can be a manager? But you have to be part of a firm to be an agent. And even if it is a boutique-y agency, it's still an agency, so there's that legitimacy.

Use your gut and good judgment when picking your agent. Don't go to a huge agency like William Morris or CAA (Creative Artists Agency) and expect that you, or anyone starting out, can get a meeting. That shouldn't be your goal anyway. Instead, go to some boutique agencies. Meet with several of them and see what they can do for you. See who else they've represented whose career you might want to emulate. I got really lucky because I got recommended to this small agency that has a really awesome young people's department. They took care of me and took care of my family and provided awesome guidance.

When finding an agent, the most important thing is to use your common sense. Ask around. Don't go to anyone who asks for money off the top. The best way to find a small agency is to be recommended to one by another person who had either been with them or knew about them.

**You have to dream big.**

Then they'll begin having you going out for things. Maybe huge movie auditions are your end goal, but remember that everyone starts somewhere. Be willing to start with PSAs (public service announcements) and local commercials. I don't say don't dream big. You have to dream big. But you have to be wise about what to do first.

## MAKING A LIFE

### THE DIFFERENCE BETWEEN SUPPORTIVE PARENTS AND "STAGE PARENTS"

It's funny, because I had a positive experience as a kid actor. But my mom has asked me what I would do if my own children (when I have them) said they wanted to go into acting. And I don't think I would let them! I don't know if most kids are cut out for it. I don't mean to sound elitist; what I mean is, it's tough. I wouldn't suggest it if you're under fifteen.

My brother started when he was a kid, and he gave up by the time he was fifteen because it's hard. You get rejected every day! A lot of it has to do with personality. There is that rare kid who has naturally thick skin and dedication. But I would not ever suggest it for anyone who isn't expecting a rough journey. You have to keep your eye on the goal and not let anything deter you.

It was a battle at the beginning, trying to get my mom to let me try to act professionally. It was bold of her to say "Yes," even after I pleaded and pleaded. She gave in, eventually, because she saw where my heart was and knew I was going to stay dedicated. There's a fine balance between pushing and just being supportive. She told me I could stop whenever I wanted. But as long as I was doing it, I had to try my hardest. She said, "You have to go full out. That's the only way. If you ever want to stop, just say the word and you're out—you never have to go on another audition again. But if this is something you want to do, you're going to go to classes and you're going to go to every audition they send you on."

Ultimately, though, the drive to do it has to be coming from the kid and not the mom. Kid actors get a bad rap, but it's usually the parents. It's not only stage moms, but stage dads, too. I don't blame child actors for being so weird and so needy, because that's how they were raised. The parents are like freaks of nature. You can quote me on that!

Obviously, there are cool kid actors, too. They're the ones who developed a passion when they were five or six and the parents allow them to follow it. But the cool ones don't generally come from the families who gave up their lives in another state and dropped everything to move to L.A. to follow this nearly unattainable dream for their kid. That's where it starts to be weird.

There's a reason why there's a stereotype for those child actors who end up in rehab. Look at someone who actually has the talent, Lindsay Lohan.

Her mom is clearly a total stage mom. And Lindsay does not know how to interact with people and live her life appropriately. That's an example where the drive to do it was probably mutual between mother and daughter, but she still led that sort of very typical child-actor life, and it never has good results.

You can see the stress on those kids. I did a commercial one time for Sprint, and we filmed a week in Palm Springs. I got to take a week off from school, and to this day, I consider it one of my top five most fun times ever. My mom and I were like, "Oh my God, we're in Palm Springs! This is so great!" There was this other kid who was in the commercial, and the poor kid was so stressed out the whole time. My mom kept telling me, "Something's wrong there."

Evil stage moms push their children into it from babyhood. I'm sorry, I've never met a six-month-old who can make their own decision about what they want to do as a career. As the kids begin supporting the family financially, the parents have to keep pushing them. It's already a lot of pressure just trying to get a job when it's something you WANT to do. Having to get a job to support your family would just be terror for a child. I've never met a child actor who had been pushed into it who is well-adjusted. And then you don't get to go to school, so it's this weird dynamic where the parent is their main friend. If they do have other friends, the other friends are usually actors, and it's this weird competitive thing. They don't get to experience true friendship for the sake of friendship, just to have a playmate. It's very calculating—the kids are saying, "Oh, this person booked this job and this job." Ewwww!

**I've never met a child actor who had been pushed into [acting] who is well-adjusted.**

A lot of kids who act are homeschooled. It's funny because my mom is a teacher, and I still couldn't imagine having my mom as my teacher. It's too many relationships at once, if your mom is your mom, your teacher, your friend, and your manager. It's like, do I call her Mom? Do I call her Mrs. Sher, the manager? Do I call her Ivy?

## PLAYING UGLY: A PRETTY SMART THING TO DO

I would never deny that there's a lot of me in Sue Heck, my character on *The Middle*. There's also a lot that's nothing like me, a lot that is totally the character. But I'm the one physically embodying her, so of course some of me is going to go into her.

Maybe Sue is rubbing off on me, too, because her optimism has become a big part of what I'm about now. I can't think of one downside to playing her. Because she looks so different than I do, I can go out in public. I wear a completely different style of clothes than she does, which is probably part of it. But, okay, maybe it really is the braces, because even if my face looks the same, people aren't expecting me to be cute at all. I can pretty much do all the stuff I want to do and not get hassled. I'm never recognized in public, even when I'm having brunch with Patty Heaton, my mom on *The Middle*, who is recognized everywhere she goes.

I hope my vibe reflects my real age, rather than the age I play on TV. No one expects to have a sort of mature person walk through the door. Once at a Critics' Choice Awards show, I was super dressed up, and I have to say, I looked pretty hot. A few of the reporters on the red carpet didn't recognize me at all. They were like, "Why am I interviewing you?" and my publicist would tell them, "She's nominated! This is Eden Sher, who plays Sue Heck on *The Middle*"—and they were so shocked. And it was such a good feeling! I thought, "Oh wow, I'm totally unrecognizable." As they say in the biz, "I traaaahns-form into Sue Heck!"

In my future, I'm probably not going to get the privilege of being uglier on TV than I am in person. I think it is bizarre when people are afraid of being geeky on TV—not

> **I would always, always, always opt for the uglier role, because for one thing, it's just more fun.**

just looking physically ugly, but being the antithesis of cool. People do not want to be uncool on TV. I would always, always, always opt for the uglier role, because for one thing, it's just more fun. You have the freedom to do anything comedically without feeling restricted by having to be in flattering clothes or worry about makeup or being shot at certain angles. And two, I don't care how vain this is: It is always awesome when people say, "Oh my God, I can't believe how ugly they make you look. You're so pretty in person!"

I hope nobody feels guilty about laughing at Sue Heck. I wouldn't be doing my job if they did. I know what you're saying. Maybe if she were in the real world, and not in comedy world, she would be much more pitiable. She'd be a little bit more of a sad character. But maybe not! I would hope that that spirit carries through and people root for her, as opposed to feeling sad when she doesn't make it. I think they're kind of going along with her spirit, thinking, "If you don't make it, it's cool, 'cause you're gonna make the next one!"

## OVERCOMING OVERTHINKING

I'm a more jovial person when I'm working. On my way to work, I sort of zone into Sue Heck music. I turn off the Sufjan Stevens and the Dirty Projectors and I put on Justin Bieber and Spice Girls and Kelly Clarkson. It makes me happy! I wouldn't want every one of Sue Heck's qualities. But there are a good number that I think are awesome, and influential on me as I play her.

I know this sounds anti-acting to say, but Sue's the kind of character that's easy to overthink. And when you overthink, you lose something. If you think about why she's doing what she's doing too hard, you'll just go in circles, and you won't find a real justification for her happiness. And that kind of happiness and cockeyed optimism, it doesn't come from a place of logic and reason, but from somewhere really deep down in the gut.

Actually, there was one scene in season one, the birthday episode, that was a turning point for me in playing her. The family forgot her birthday, and I was supposed to be really, really disappointed and upset, and then, in a heartbeat, like turning on a dime, be totally ecstatic again, because they agree to go on a family trip. As we were shooting it, it became clear I wasn't getting it. I was trying to justify it so hard in my head as an actor: "Okay, what's going on right now? What thought is going through her head that would make me/her switch? What exactly am I thinking?"

I talked to the director about it, and he said, "Uh-uh. You're not thinking about *anything*. You were sad, and then you find out you're going on the trip, and you are so happy, and that is it. If you think too hard about it, it's not going to make sense." And he totally changed my world. I realized that

**Maybe Sue is rubbing off on me, too, because her optimism has become a big part of what I'm about now.**

it has nothing to do with rationalizing behavior. It doesn't have to do with anything. It just is what it is. And since then, I've felt so much more free. I feel like I've been able to do funnier things, because there's no need to justify it. You just have to *be*.

It sounds sort of cheesy, but also since that pivotal moment, I have been even more uberinspired by Sue Heck. Because what that director told me was actually genius advice. If you're sad, and then you get good news, why on earth *would* you wallow in the sadness when you can choose to be happy about the better news that was just given to you? ★

For more from Eden go to
http://www.nowyoutellmebooks.com/actors.

# MICHAEL MCKEAN

## "Insist on having fun."

Although a good chunk of Michael McKean's acting résumé is made up of unctuous authority figures, his best-known role remains the dim, deeply unaware rocker David St. Hubbins, lead singer of everyone's favorite fictional rock 'n' roll band, Spinal Tap.

He started out with the Credibility Gap, a satirical troupe that included Harry Shearer and David L. Lander. McKean and Lander became Lenny and Squiggy on the 70s sitcom *Laverne & Shirley*, which led to the film *This Is Spinal Tap*, one of Michael's many collaborations with Christopher Guest, who later directed him in semi-improvisational films such as *The Big Picture*, *Best in Show* and *A Mighty Wind*. (The latter film got McKean and his wife, Annette O'Toole, an Oscar nomination for Best Song.) Most recently, he's shifted his emphasis to the stage, beginning early in the 2000s, when he was invited to take over for Harvey Fierstein as Edna in the original Broadway run of *Hairspray*. He recently played Gloucester opposite Sam Waterston's King Lear.

# MAKING A LIVING

## YOU ARE MOST MARKETABLE BEING YOURSELF

I did this funny little seminar at a casting convention. The class was made up of kids getting into the business as well as older people who'd been working as extras and wanted to be actors. Besides fielding the usual questions ("How do I get an agent?" and "Is my head shot okay?"), I tried to come up with some words of wisdom. The only profound thing I had to say was: if you look in the mirror and waste any time at all wishing you were more like somebody else, then maybe acting isn't what you want to do. Maybe what you want to do is something unrelated to the arts.

For example, it's the early fifties, you're just getting out of the army, you don't really have any clear ideas of how to design your future. You're a little below average in height and not conventionally handsome, and you've got a speech impediment and a glass eye. Should you become an actor? Well, if you're Peter Falk, that's exactly what you should do. But did Peter Falk spend any time looking in a mirror and saying, "Man, I wish I looked a little more like John Garfield?" Not a minute. He went out as himself, with this funny eye and everything else; and he's one of the most brilliant actors we've ever had in this country, period. Just gold, this guy! You look at his work in *The Brink's Job* and *All the Marbles*, and these are the most amazing performances. *Husbands*, he's brilliant in. He's also a television star of some note. But if he let his looks or manner or lack of polish deter him, we all would've been tremendously cheated—him first of all.

> **The more you are like someone else, the less work you are going to find.**

The more you are like someone else, the less work you are going to find. It seems paradoxical, because people are always making themselves the next so-and-so, and sometimes do very well at it. But if they can only get your product at your outlet, you get the sale. So it's not just a good idea to be yourself, it's a good business strategy. Who fought over all those Arnold Stang parts? Nobody! Arnold Stang walked in and got them all. Well, I guess Marvin Kaplan got a few.

## YOU HAVE NOTHING TO FEAR BUT THE STATUS QUO

Before you're established, you'll have to audition because nobody knows who you are. If you're like me and you have more than one look, and therefore can play more than one kind of part, sometimes you have to audition, too. And there are some directors who make it a policy to always "see people," which means you have to audition or you at least have to submit a tape.

The process of auditioning when you're first starting out is nerve-racking to some people. Why? It's fear! But it's never been clear to me what you're really afraid of. When I've spoken to young actors, I ask them to examine why that is.

One lie they tell themselves is, "Oh, that's just the energy I need to do that scene." Well, maybe it's technically true, but then why do you feel as if you're going to throw up if this is just acting juice?

Then I ask, "What are you really nervous about? Why are you afraid? Are they going to *harm* you? What's the worst thing they can do?" And they think for a minute and they always answer: "Not give me the job." And I say, "Yeah. Guess what? You already

**What's the worst thing that can happen at an audition? You don't get the job? Well, guess what? You already don't have the job! So you don't have anything to lose."**

don't have the job! You're going in there, and the other shoe has dropped already. So there's really no point in being afraid of not getting the job. That is a done deal. Go in there and just do whatever comes into your head. Stay loose, make choices if it's appropriate, and if you're supposed to be a leprechaun, you've gotta fake the Irish accent a little bit. But be as unfettered by fear as you can be, because you have nothing to lose. The ax has already fallen." That's my thinking about auditioning, and it resonates with actors. I don't know whether they put it into practice or not. I try to.

## SELF-CASTING AGAINST TYPE

After I played the villain in *The Brady Bunch Movie*, I got a lot of offers to play the guy who gets dumped on at the end of the movie—the guy who's the nemesis of whatever person the audience loves and identifies with, usually a boss or a high school principal or dean. Nothing was tempting at all about the scripts. It got to the point where I would get the script and glimpse the character and then go to the end to see what substance he winds up covered with, whether it's excrement or vomit or marshmallow fluff. That stuff got so familiar so fast that I try to avoid that kind of thing.

A lot of it has to do with the order in which I do projects. I like following one type of character with something very different, and I've managed to do that. It's only visible if you look at my credits, and nobody does that except me. But I do like to look at my filmography and see: well, this character was a lot different from this guy, and this one was a lot different from this one. If I have two in a row that are alike—the hard-ass principal at this high school and the hard-ass boss—I think I should've broken those up a bit. I saw early on that this was something to pay attention to. So after I did *Laverne & Shirley*, the next thing I did was a movie called *Young Doctors in Love* in which I played the straight man, this blond stiff, while everyone around me was a loony. It was very, very different from what I had done on *Laverne & Shirley*. And then *Spinal Tap* was the next thing that came out.

> **It isn't your first gig that typecasts you. It's the second gig.**

It isn't your first gig that typecasts you. It's the second gig. So somebody who comes out of playing one type of character and does a couple more jobs where it's that same kind of thing, you've basically put up a sign saying that's what you do. And it's never a good idea. Imagine if Sean Penn had followed *Fast Times at Ridgemont*

*High* with a couple more movies about Spicoli, the stoned surfer, or his type. In fact, I'm sure Sean got offered *Maui Wowie: The Motion Picture.* Sean Penn is a really good actor who had a great take on this character. But if he'd just stayed there and phoned in the same performance movie after movie, he would have become like Francis the Talking Mule. So, like I say, it ain't your first break that types you. It's redoing that same break in the same way.

I try not to take any parts where I don't think there's anything there, or if nothing occurs to me, or if it's not inspiring in any way. But I also think that there's probably a way to be okay at anything—and to have fun doing anything. If there's something to be done and it looks like fun, I insist on having fun.

## REGRET DOES NOT HAVE TO BE A SOB STORY

There've been some big jobs that I didn't get; and even if whoever did get that part went on and had a big career, it never really bothers me. A part should be something you throw into the hopper and you get rid of rather than something you obsess about in hindsight. Remember all those people who wanted to be Catwoman?

I had a friend once who called me up in tears. She has dogs that are like her family. And she was so distraught, I thought, "Oh my God, one of her beloved family member dogs has dropped dead! Oh, how am I going to deal with this? I've got to be a friend here." Eventually, she was able to pull herself together enough to tell me that she lost a part to this other actress who was her archrival. And I went, "If you're so broken up that I thought someone died, then something's not right."

There are always some regrets. But regretting doesn't hurt. You can go ahead and regret them. When I was a teenager, there were a lot of girls whom I really would have loved to have had another shot at. But I also see that it probably would've changed everything. You can't backpedal in real life, so why do it in your fantasy life, or even just the world of your thoughts, which amounts to the same thing?

The people I worked with on *Laverne & Shirley* created a new show. And they called me up and said, "You are perfect for this. You have to do this." I read the pilot, and at that time it was called *We Don't Have a Title Yet*—that's what it said on the script. It was their brainchild. "We've got a deal, we're on air, but we don't have the guy." I read it, and it was very funny; but I thought the character was too close to what I had just come from with *Laverne & Shirley,* kind of a dumb slob. So I said it's not for me. They went on and did the show, and it was *Married With Children.* And I thought, "Well, that show wouldn't have been a hit with me." With anybody but Ed O'Neill, that show would've been "Eh . . . next." He was perfect. Maybe the show would've been a hit anyway, but it wouldn't have been as good a show, because he was so the guy.

By the same token I was offered another show where I thought, "This is good; this might actually run," but the part I was offered was the dad on the show. In fact, the show did have a good run. But if I'd signed on, I'd have been committed to a sitcom that ran for four years—where my character never got a laugh. I'd just come in and feed a straight line to a star. Truth is, nobody remembers who the dad was on that show. So I don't regret not doing it, although it would've been nice to have that kind of cash for four years.

## THE STAGE AS SMALL TOWN AND UNIVERSE

Working on the stage has been a big change for me. I've worked a lot in New York and London and Chicago and now L.A., and I'm having an awfully good time. Theater was what I set out to do in the first place. People are as much fun and as nice and as kind of needy as I'd imagined they would be when I was doing theater back in high school.

My first Broadway musical was *Hairspray.* I'd been in the show for about one day before I knew I wanted to be in more companies like this, full of really great, supportive, cool people—most of them a lot younger than me.

This was kind of telling: I did *South Pacific* at the Hollywood Bowl three years ago, and it was really fun. For one thing, I got to hear Brian Stokes

Mitchell sing "This Nearly Was Mine" every night for four nights, and it was fabulous. The show was partially staged—more like a concert with acting—which is what they do at the Bowl. I was playing Luther Billis, which is a great comic part. And I got away with it. At the Hollywood Bowl, the nearest people to you seem as if they're about fifty yards away, so you can be sixty years old and play a guy who's in the navy. There's something in general about the stage that is more forgiving than film or TV. Usually, I'm playing people my age. But there's something about the stage, from an audience's point of view, that lets you fudge. Which is great.

Being in a theater company is like entering a benign state. There's usually a feeling among the actors that we're all in this together. People who aren't decent to others get isolated pretty quickly. The show is live: you're creating it as you go along every single night, and you're all in that same boat. You're only as good as you are that moment. If you go out onstage and you don't have a prop that you need because the whole scene is about this pen you pull out of your pocket, you've made a terrible error—and everyone can, and will, make those errors. But it gives a kind of a trapeze-act feel of danger to live performances, which is great.

**[Live theater] gives a kind of a trapeze-act feel of danger to performances, which is great.**

I recently had a chance to do *Our Town* for sixty shows in New York. There were about twenty-five people in the cast, and we all shared one large dressing room. A lot of them had been doing the show for nineteen months already when I came in. It was a real community. They were the most amazing people. I felt that right away in *Hairspray*, too. The majority of the cast had been together for two years already, by which time a lot of those kids had had different affairs and relationships. It was like moving to a small town. *Our Town* was the most blatant example of that, of really good people, all equipped with egos and sore spots, but primarily there for one another because that's the job. *Our Town* is a play about a small town that is, of course, a play about the universe. At its best, any community is a workable model of the universe, and theater supplies that in a nice way.

In film and TV, there's exterior pressure about getting it right, because it costs ten thousand dollars a minute, and you feel it. It's just a bigger deal on a money level. In the theater, the people who put up the money expect to lose it. And guess what? They quite often do. It'd be nice if it paid better for the actors and if it cost less for the patrons, because a hundred and twenty dollars is a lot to pay for a ticket to see anything. Even if the show you see is ten times better than a movie, it's still a lot of money. But thank God, people who love the theater keep supporting it.

## RESPECT EVERYBODY ELSE'S METHOD . . . WHETHER OR NOT IT'S *THE* METHOD

I knew a guy in college who said something that surprised me in its stupidity, but it also stayed with me. He said, "My goal is to become as good an actor as Peter O'Toole. Then I'll be okay." I didn't say anything at the time, but I thought, "Why Peter O'Toole? Because he's your favorite actor? He's the best actor in the world? [Probably the fellow thought that was the case.] But why bring *him* into this? And secondly, do you really have a plateau in mind of how good you're going to be? What an irrelevancy! I mean, I've worked with you, and you've got a lot more to learn than how high your artistic ambition goes."

The craft of acting is about discovering how close to real life acting is, and should be—and then forgetting it. Next, work on all the physicality. Work on finding the light and not standing in the other guy's. Learn to respect other actors' processes. Don't lord yours over anyone. If you think an hour of yoga and an hour of meditation are the very least an actor can do, keep it to yourself. Do it—by all means, do it. We won't look for you at dinnertime! We'll know you're in there meditating and you're a wonderful actor. But everybody's got a process; everyone's got something that's good for him or her.

When I went into *Hairspray*, I trailed the show with Harvey Fierstein, whose part I was going into. And, I gotta tell you, trailing Harvey was as entertaining as that play has ever been. He dragged me along, showing me all the quick changes: "You gotta go onstage here because you can't get through there, and then you gotta jump out at her and go *Bahhhh!*" It was a play-by-play of exactly every single thing he did as part of his routine.

But then, in the middle of the play, he had twenty to thirty minutes off. And you know what he did? He watched sitcoms. DVDs of *Sanford and Son.* It never would've occurred to me, but of course you have to do that. I had only done one play on Broadway before, and I was off for some chunks of that; and I usually just hung around backstage, because I thought that's what you do. But if you're in something for two years, you're not gonna sweat out the rest of the play. If you've got twenty minutes off, you can go do something.

Don't ever make up your mind about what a suitable process should be for something you've never done.

## WHEN YOU GET THE JOB, HAVE YOUR LEARNING ANTENNAE UP

Recently my wife, Annette, and I watched an episode of *Gunsmoke*, which was the first acting she'd ever done on film. She was eighteen years old, working with Harry Morgan, who is going to outlive us all. (You realize that Harry Morgan and Abe Vigoda are going to be the only people left on the earth, bless their hearts.) Anyway, she's unbelievably beautiful, of course; but every now and then she's hidden behind another actor, or she'll be talking to someone and all you see is hair. I was about to point it out and she said, "Yeah, this is where I learned those basics. When I did that episode of *Gunsmoke*, people were telling me things like 'Honey, you should be sure that you can see the camera, because that means the camera can see you.' This part was shot before I learned, and this is why you're only seeing half of me behind Harry Morgan."

Many, many things you will learn as you go. Some of the learning is incredibly tedious because the others on the set aren't there to teach you; they're there to do their job. When the continuity person comes over to you for the first time and tells you, "If your hand is on the table here, it can't be up here in the close-up" and has to explain it to you, don't feel bad; just decide you're going to be a quick study. Remember that when you're filming, to make scenes match you have to do exactly the same thing in every take. Then remember what you've learned, and do it for the rest of your life.

So pay attention when you're first learning the ropes, and don't forget the ropes.

## MAKING A LIFE

### MARRIAGE AND MUTUAL CAREERS

With married actor couples there's always a little *A Star Is Born* lurking somewhere. You're sure one of you is heading for the top and the other will never work again. (And somehow you'll each feel that you spend a disproportionate amount of time in the second category.) But wait! You don't have to walk out into the sea to drown or slap anybody at the Oscars.

> **With married actor couples there's always a little *A Star Is Born* lurking somewhere.**

My only advice is a cautionary tale. There was a couple who were at one of the colleges I went to, acting students and sweethearts of the drama class. They were great looking, a slightly funkier version of Barbie and Ken. Beautiful people. They fell in love, got married while still in college, immediately got cast as a couple on a soap, signed five-year contracts—and then immediately broke up. So they had to be America's sweethearts while not getting along well enough to stay married. I always thought, "*That's* probably a bigger nightmare than a few squabbles over who's making more money." So if you can avoid that one . . .

It all depends on personalities. Eleven years ago I married a working actress, and we both like to work, and we both work all the time. Because Annette and I are both steadily employed, at least some of the time we can make decisions without looking at the dollar figure. We can kind of switch off. I'll make a few bucks and do something on TV while she does her play in New York, and then we switch and go off to Chicago while I do a play because working at Steppenwolf means a lot to me. Sometimes it's kind of hard to remember where we are, but it's also fun.

It helps that we have the same manager, who helps us coordinate and always copies everything for both of us. When we have to choose between projects, we help each other melt the decisions down into the basics: how much output there for how much input here—things like that. It's pretty pragmatic, and not so much a game plan as more of a system of analysis of possibilities. Which I must've gotten from her side of the family, because I've never been terribly well organized. I'm a lot better now, or else she would've thrown me out.

Annette and I have nurtured "couple habits" to a certain extent. We play cards and play casino once a day, and we have other little rituals. We love walking the dog together. She is one of the most settled people I know. Not stubborn—she's always open to new ideas and has an amazing intellect—but she likes the comfort of a routine. And it helps with things such as living apart or having to commute to see each other or even just hanging out and dealing with stuff together. Having some kind of ritualistic, normal thing going on is a good remedy for friction you might feel professionally.

A couple of months ago Annette realized she hadn't worked in a while. A theatrical thing came up, and she thought she had a shot at it. But they cast somebody very different. Annette started thinking, "Maybe I'll change careers! Maybe I'll start knitting professionally." And she hears the equivalent from me: "I just want to sit here for the rest of my life and play music and learn recording techniques." Then she does a TV show, works really hard on it, and immediately gets offered this stage job. I have a feeling that if I remind her that it was just about a month ago when she was ready to start knitting, it wouldn't register. Because it's not an expression of any real thing. Neither of us is the retiring type. I worked with Jerry Orbach in 2001—Annette and I both did a *Law & Order* with him—and we wound up talking about,

> # When we're done, when we wrap one final time, just take us right to the graveyard and right into the hole.

does anybody actually retire? Jerry said, "It's idiotic. All of us, when we're done, when we wrap one final time, just take us right to the graveyard and right into the hole. We'll work right up until then." And he did.

A lot of plans have to do with the long range, but it's really the *short* long range. There's a lot of work I'd like to do, but it'd be idiotic of me to say what it's going to be. I don't know what I want to do when I'm seventy. If I really work out a lot, I could play King Lear, but I'm probably not going to work out. If they develop the eighty-pound Cordelia [Lear has to carry his dead daughter, Cordelia], I'll do it. Call me. ★

For more from Michael go to
http://www.nowyoutellmebooks.com/actors.

# ALEXANDRA NEIL

## "Realize what you have to offer."

Alexandra Neil's acting career has been varied. She's performed in a number of plays, including *Rock 'n' Roll* and *Match* on Broadway. Her films include *Twelve*, *Afterschool*, and *Something's Gotta Give*. Alexandra is often recognized for her work on soap operas such as *One Life to Live*, *Guiding Light*, *As the World Turns*, and *Texas*.

She's taught at Michael Howard Studios, the MFA program at Brooklyn College, and at the National Theater Institute. She now teaches her own class in New York City.

# MAKING A LIVING

## TRAINING FIRST!

You wouldn't want a brain surgeon who hasn't been trained operating on your brain. You wouldn't want an architect who didn't study building your house. I find it extremely depressing when someone crosses my path who has just decided to be an actor, and this person's first priority is to get head shots and an agent. I'm amazed at how many people think it's a decision to be made as opposed to a craft to be learned and worked on. That's self-defeating for them, an exercise in depression and frustration. Of course, some people are unbelievably beautiful, and chances are they'll walk into an acting class for the first time already having a modeling agent. But that doesn't make them actors.

Acting is a craft. It takes years to develop technique so you know what you're doing when you work. That doesn't mean you can't work as you learn. I feel as if I'm constantly studying and will be for the rest of my life. I don't think there's ever a point where you know it all. But to know nothing, and to just go headlong into the business aspect of it without looking at the craft part, would make you look like probably less than who you really are. If you start class already having an agent, you've got to do the best you can to catch up, because at auditions you're going to be competing with people who've had great training.

Can you go into acting without training? Some people have incredible instincts, and sometimes a performance on film can be shaped in the editing room and by the director leading you through certain things. But certainly not in a play. Live theater separates those people out of the pack. You have to have technique to be able to do theater. Even if you were to do a film and be wonderful in it once because of your instincts, at a certain point, lack of training catches up with you. I saw that happen when I did soap operas. A lot of those young actors aren't in the business anymore, whereas the actors who really trained, who committed to the technique of acting, are still doing really well.

Technique is what will save you when you're in trouble. If everything is going wonderfully in a natural way and things are flowing out of you freely, that's fantastic—and hopefully most people have experienced that a few times in their lives. But if things aren't clicking or you have no chemistry with your partner or the director and you can't communicate and you feel lost and confused and you have no idea

> **Technique is what will save you when you're in trouble.**

what's going on and you feel like you're terrible, that's when you need the craft. Then you can say, "Well, let me go back through the things I know and see where I can help myself."

## YOUR AGENT AS LIFE PARTNER

It's important to find an agent who really gets you. When I was younger, I spent a lot of my time with agents who categorized me in a way that wasn't really useful and that was very limiting. I finally found an agent who appreciated my mind and also was willing to see me in less conventional ways. I did two Broadway shows, and all kinds of things changed because my agent really saw me. Before that I had agents who weren't right for me—some good, some not so good. I sometimes had interesting ones, but it was like dating a lot of people. Not really dating them—more like *marrying* a lot of people and then not really finding your soul mate till much later. And I think you should look for your soul mate in an agent—somebody who really can know you as well and who appreciates your strengths. I don't think you should settle or think, "Well, this person thinks I'm marketable only as x or y, but I can change his mind."

Find someone who really sees things about you that are not apparent on the surface and who is curious enough to invest time to get to know you more, who will call you and say, "This is a wacky idea, but would you like to go in for this? Is that something that's exciting to you?" That's what you need to look for. It's made all the difference for me, and I wish I had known that earlier. It's so freeing and so fantastic when you find that person,

**All kinds of things changed because my [new] agent really saw me.**

because then you have a real partnership as opposed to the role that most actors play with agents—which is really just the role of supplicant. You're waiting for the phone to ring and then you're waiting for your agent to tell you who you are. There are other ways to have that relationship, but you've got to have the courage to look for someone who doesn't sell you short.

For example, if you're dying to do theater and the agent leaves that out of the mix, that's not the right agent for you. I had always done theater—a lot of regional theater as well as a lot of workshops and off-Broadway in New York. But my current agents took my theater career seriously and took it to another level. They don't limit my options just so they can collect the commission.

## GO EAST, YOUNG STAGE ACTOR

I'm a complete die-hard New York person. I went to L.A. twice, worked both times, and loved it. It was for brief amounts of time, and both times I suddenly got called back to New York for jobs, so I think I was just meant to be here. I certainly wouldn't hold my career up to be some example of a perfect career. But if theater is part of who you are and you love it and you must do it, I suppose New York is the place.

And from the theater you can get jobs in TV and film, because people will see you in a play and then they'll call you into their office. It works that way here; I'm not so sure it works that way in L.A. In fact, if you're in New York and you don't do any theater, it's a little bit strange. Of course, if you're doing workshops or off-Broadway theater, you have to supplement your income. Most actors here want to work in all the mediums. Everybody loves mixing it up and moving from one medium to another and seeing what the differences are and what's interesting about that.

The first time I was on Broadway, in *Match*, I worked as an understudy. I got lucky and went on often in a three-character play, a lot of which was really a two-character play—and my partner was Frank Langella. I learned so much from that experience, and I'm grateful to him forever. The second time I was in a Tom Stoppard play called *Rock 'n' Roll*, which was phenomenal, too.

I didn't have much vocal technique until I was older. In my forties I studied quite a bit with Patsy Rodenberg, who's a legendary Shakespeare and voice teacher. She helped me find power, because I suddenly developed a lot more of a vocal presence, which helped me expand theatrically.

## HOW TO BE CHOOSY

This happens a lot: you'll sit around for a few months, and suddenly you'll get two or three jobs, and you have to choose one. Often in that situation, I've gone into complete panic mode. It's hard not to. But it's better if you can really just take a step back and breathe and look really hard at who you are in this point in your life and what you really want. I would advise people to do it on a case-by-case basis—not to panic, not to rush into any kind of a decision if they're not sure, to talk with everybody they know whom they trust. You literally should make a column A and a column B, pros and cons . . . and ultimately just go with what your gut says.

When I was really young, I got offered a part as a replacement in a Broadway play that had had a long run but was kind of on its last legs. At the same time, I got an offer to play Cherie in *Bus Stop* at Actors Theatre of Louisville. I chose Louisville. People would say, "Were you crazy? Why wouldn't you want a Broadway credit in your early twenties?" But I didn't regret it—I loved every minute of that production and that experience. It probably wasn't the definitive *Bus Stop*, and I don't even know if I was any good in it; but it was a huge growing experience for me. And I would be very sad if that role had been left out of my biography because I made some sort of a commercial choice.

## HOW NOT TO BE CHOOSY

One thing that I regret is that I turned down a number of jobs for reasons that ended up being not important. I'm always quick to say, "Oh, I'm not gonna do that." But sometimes it's just good to keep working. If you have momentum and you're working steadily, and then suddenly something comes your way and you think, it's not up to my standards," or "the part isn't that interesting; I've done this before"—those are all reasons that I've turned down jobs—it might be better to just keep doing work.

Work begets work. The more you're working, the more you develop a kind of momentum, which can be stopped when you turn things down. I've experienced that a few times. When you're riding that sort of momentum, it's better to stay with it. If jobs are coming your way, it's better to try to find reasons to do them than to try to find reasons not to do them.

> **It's better to try to find reasons to [take acting jobs] than to try to find reasons not to take them.**

If you're in that realm where you get offered an awful lot of high quality stuff, then, yes, of course, be picky. But if you're like most of my friends, a working actor but not a star, it's a little different. Often, in television, the size of the role changes after you've been hired. They'll add scenes, or they'll have something in mind that's not really included in the audition. And you have to trust what they're telling you, what the role is, and that they'll be true to their word. It could end up being something substantial, where you can make a mark in that episode. You'd be working with amazing people and it would be worth doing. It's happened to me; I've turned something down and a few weeks later my husband says, "I saw that part that you turned down, and it was a really good part!"

## QUICKIES CAN BE FUN

If you're going in to do a guest star or guest lead on a series, it can be really great just to spend a week with those people, and hang out with them so intensely and have all these experiences with them that are probably extremely intimate and weird. If in the script your husband is sleeping with your daughter, for example, and you're in the room with all of them living that life, it can really be freeing and wonderful to know that this is my week of going into this world. After that, it's going to be over. So I'm just going to dive in as fully as I can and have this experience. I think you couldn't sustain those kinds of *Law & Order*-type guest star parts for a long time. They're always so intensely weird. The characters are really traumatized, so they couldn't be on the show week after week because they'd be dead. But to dive into something and sink your teeth into it that way for a week with really great collaborators can be thrilling.

## THE UNPREDICTABILITY OF AUDITIONS

I'm terrible at auditioning. I struggle with it every day and have my whole entire career. I think it's really hard and terrifying. The most you can try and do is be as present as possible, and sometimes that seems like an insurmountable task; but that's the best possible thing. Be present, and also be prepared—prepared in the sense that you know what you want to do, but you're open—so that if they throw something your way, you're not locked down into some kind of rigid thinking.

# MAKING A LIFE

## IF YOU THINK YOU COULD DO SOMETHING ELSE . . . DO

I do think that to be in it for the long haul you have to love acting so deeply and so passionately that you really can't imagine yourself doing anything else. There are a lot of ups and downs, and it's a very trying existence sometimes. Not even just the rejection, but all the waiting is so painful and so hard. If you have a craft to sustain you, if you had a passion for the work, if you're immersed in the world of the theater—and by theater I mean all of it—you can have a wonderful life. But if there's even a piece of you where you feel like, "Gee, I wish I had gone to grad school and been this or that," then it's probably better that you go do that. It's hard—I mean, it's really hard. My accountant stays in his office during tax time twenty hours a day and he's an accountant, so just think how hard an actor has to work.

That doesn't mean you should be single-minded about it. My advice would be to try not to be neurotic in any way; and if you feel that you are neurotic, then go get some help. You need to be a healthy person to do this so that your ego won't be blown in one direction or another by events that are happening to you. You need some perspective and a steady rudder as you negotiate the ups and downs. Having a career that's going to have some longevity involves having a really grounded perspective on life and on yourself, and having connections to the world—stuff that you do in order to share and to give back. But if you're in some sort of bubble where you're just an actor . . . I don't know many people like that, frankly. I would think you would end up having some sort of breakdown.

People who are narcissists exist in any career, in any walk of life, in any potential family or job or situation. I don't think actors necessarily have more narcissism than painters or symphony conductors or even mathematicians or lawyers. The actors that I know are the most generous, the smartest, the most interesting, the most fun people on the planet—and very selfless, supportive, and kind. I mean, it's a wonderful thing to do with your life—not the easiest thing, but incredibly wonderful. And the colleagues that you'll meet will be such substantial people. There's nothing slight or "less than" to me about being an actor. It's a very true way to exist in the world.

## QUIT YOUR DAY JOB . . . IF IT'S KILLING YOU

It's so hard right now to be a young actor in New York, unless you've got a trust fund or something. You arrive here, and the odds are astronomical beyond belief, and you have to room with several people, and just coming up with the rent every month is such a burden for so many people. I see young actors burning themselves out. Sometimes it's in safe jobs, like an office job where they'll never get out to audition, so it's just futile to be living this existence, but they're afraid to let go of the security. With other people it's incredibly long hours catering, bartending, waitressing, and doing exhausting work—and showing up for auditions and for class dragging and exhausted and burned out from their "day job." That to me is so sad and difficult. The reason they're here is to be actors, and they need to figure out a life that will give them enough energy to pursue what they want to do and still make money. The more innovative you can be about it, and the more you can think highly of yourself in terms of, "Yes, I do deserve to make a hundred bucks an hour," the better.

One student of mine hostesses at events; and each event pays a lot of money, so she only has to do it three or four times a month. She's very beautiful, but so are so many people in my class. She always has energy and always has this sparkle in her eyes; she takes care of herself really well. She said, "Oh, I just figured it out. I was waitressing, and it was just so crazy. And then I figured out: 'No, wait; there are other ways'." I think for everybody there's something. You can be someone's personal assistant. You can babysit. You can do web design or another job where you make your own schedule. There *are* other jobs. The people I find who are free enough to pursue their careers and their crafts are not burdened by really exhausting day jobs.

Most of the actors I know have been to college, and many to grad school, and majored in very interesting things and have so much to offer the world. The ones I see who negotiate this best find jobs where they're actually using a piece of themselves that's more than catering or bartending. In this other life that they have, they approach it creatively and as if they're worth something. There's nothing more depressing than somebody who's amazing and trained and brilliant just eeking by working at Starbucks for years. It's hard seeing them miserable when there's a possibility they could look at themselves differently and see what they have to offer and be working for much more money by creating some sort of new show for themselves or by connecting with somebody who can lead them to a situation where they can work part-time or make their own hours but still be doing something that's substantial and creative that pays better. Look for ways to make money that aren't going to exhaust you, that aren't going to deplete you or demean you, that use your strengths where you can develop skills in that realm and have that as a supplement to acting.

## HAVING A FAMILY: NO REGRETS

I was a single mom for my daughter's first eight years. I had to make a lot of choices that involved not leaving her. I never regretted any of them, and they weren't difficult because that is what I was doing: I was being Zoe's mom during that time. It was a wonderful, amazing experience. I didn't regret missing this or that job, and I never have. You can't weigh the two things. They're just not comparable. Work is fantastic, but you're never going to blame your child for not going and doing that movie—it just doesn't feel like that. You make the choices you make based on what your life is like at the moment. If you have a child, a child is going to grow up fast and leave. My daughter's in college now, and I suddenly can go and do regional theater for the first time in twenty years. Those kinds of things come around again. When you have children, it's not really hard to prioritize or to choose. It just sort of happens for you.

## IT SHOULD BE SCARY

I think every good job I've had has been a real challenge. Sometimes the best ones are the ones where you think in the beginning, "Oh God, I'm never going to be able to do this!" I know that feeling of having an unbelievably intense challenge where you don't know if you can really do it; you don't know if you can come out the other side of it. And every time I've felt that, those things have been my best experiences by far. My teacher Michael Howard says, "They pay to see us in danger. They don't pay to see us be safe." And I think there's something about an actor putting himself or herself in danger that translates to the audience. It's very exciting.

> **[Audiences] pay to see us in danger. They don't pay to see us be safe.**

I don't mean some sort of physical, shady danger. I mean in terms of taking chances and going out on a limb and being in a realm that you haven't been in before in the work. If I were trying to choose between a job that was challenging and one that was not, at this point in my life I definitely would take the challenging job. Because even if you fail, it is so rewarding, ultimately.

## WHAT GOOD IS SITTING ALONE IN YOUR ROOM?

I think the biggest danger is sitting in your apartment waiting for your phone to ring and letting that be the defining mode of your existence. It's happened to me, and to everyone I know, but I believe in fighting it.

There are so many ways that you can act besides doing a television show or being in a play. You can write something and produce it yourself. You can go to Africa and do theater with people in a village where it's going to change their lives, and yours, forever. You can go to a retirement home and do a reading for people, and it will be the most amazing thing they have experienced in weeks. There are so many things you can do that will help you realize that what you have to offer is a huge gift to the world—and also, weirdly, to yourself, because it comes back to you. When you give something away, you feel better than when you're hoarding it.

It's very important for actors to look at themselves and see what their potential is to be a double threat or a triple threat or a quadruple threat: writing, directing, and producing, as well as acting. We can free ourselves from being in the supplicant role of waiting for the phone to ring by producing ourselves. Most of the actors I know are also extraordinary writers. Many of them are incredible directors. Actors usually know more about directing than a lot of people who call themselves directors! And then in terms of producing, if you have any head for business at all, you can produce your colleagues' work; you can produce yourself; you can start a company. The thing is to generate the work, to live where your passion is in terms of the work, and to develop as much as you can for the world. Also, I would encourage you to think outside the box as much as possible. I just read in the *Times* about actors who are doing Shakespeare in the subway.

I directed a documentary film, and I also wrote a play recently that's had a bit of a life, which is really exciting. I've done a lot of it in various realms, and I wish I'd done a lot more. Somebody told me years ago when *she* was fifty and I was in my twenties: "Produce yourself." And I heard it—but I didn't really hear it. Because for a while you have stars in your eyes about your "acting career," and it's hard to think of yourself as doing anything but that. But I would encourage everyone to try. Take a writing class, or get a group of your friends together and start a company and branch out and do something in your community, or go around the world and go to some place that really needs to have stories told and write those stories and direct them and act them with the people there. And then come back and see how much your phone rings. I'm pretty sure it will be a lot more. I think that what we put out there is what we get back. It really is true.

I think that what we do is spiritual in many ways. I don't think you can separate that aspect of it. There are huge gifts from the universe. Sometimes you feel you're channeling something more powerful than you are. There are so many things that happen that are "meant to be" in our business. There are so many accidents that happen onstage that end up being the best moment of the play; and, suddenly, lightning bolts come down, and you realize how magical it is. It's sort of like falling in love, you know. All these things align, and you end up where you are because of everything. That's why I think even the mistakes are not terrible. They're going to lead you where you need to be, and at any moment you can say, "I'm going to do more," and just decide to do it. You just need to know that you have some power. It's *not* a powerless career. It's not

**So many accidents that happen on stage end up being the best moment of the play.**

necessarily a place of waiting and longing. It can be a place of great action; and the more action you take, the more energy there is around you. It does come back. ★

For more from Alexandra go to
http://www.nowyoutellmebooks.com/actors.

# JOSEPH KOLINSKI

## "Moments of Absolute Ecstasy"

Joseph Kolinski has worked on Broadway, in regional theaters, and on television for the last twenty years. He was in the original Broadway casts of *Titanic*, *Les Misérables*, *The Three Musketeers*, and *The Human Comedy*, as well as in Madison Square Garden's *A Christmas Carol* and *Dance a Little Closer*. Joe was also the Celebrant in Leonard Bernstein's *Mass* for the Kennedy Center's tenth anniversary production. Soap fans may recognize him as the evil Prince Roland of Mendorra on ABC's *One Life to Live*. He lives with his wife and daughter in New York City.

# MAKING A LIVING

## NEW IN TOWN

When I came to New York from Detroit in the late seventies, the going idea was, if you were going to try to make it in New York, you needed to have about $10,000 in your pocket to see you through setting up an apartment, starting with a good voice teacher, and maybe starting acting classes. I make that as equivalent to $40,000 or $50,000 today. How many kids just out of school have access to that kind of money?

**The starving actor cliché exists for a reason.**

Most people coming to New York or Los Angeles to try their hand in the business bring debt with them, and immediately begin the process of expanding that debt. The starving actor cliché exists for a reason. If you have a rich uncle who's willing to finance your first year in the trenches, milk him. Otherwise, find a job as a waiter (preferably trained for haute cuisine) and gather as much money as you can and live as cheaply as you can. Have you heard this all before? Sorry, that's just the way it is.

I arrived in the city with about three hundred dollars in my pocket; and that was gone, as you can imagine, in a heartbeat. So began life in the red. That went on for about ten years. For one five-year stretch I got a new Broadway show every year. Believe me, that's not a bad average. Each time I got a show, I would pay down the credit cards to zero. And each time, just as I got them to zero, the show would close and I would start to build debt again.

Here's a bit of advice that no one ever gave me; maybe they thought it went without saying. You have to be very selective about where and with whom you choose to study. Keep in mind that, particularly in the arts, you must find people who can help you find *your* way. Too many want to show you their way. The cost of lessons is such a huge part of the early years; you have a right and a duty to yourself to be picky.

I'm not sure why it is, but people tend to stay with the first voice teacher they try. They also tend to stay with the first therapist that they try. In either case, they should really set up appointments with two or three different people at the outset and choose based upon their own impressions. This would save so much heartache and second-guessing down the road.

> **Find people who can help you find *your* way. Too many want to show you their way.**

Again, what you're looking for is a mentor who will help you to find *your* way.

My first voice teacher spent a year getting me to stop singing like Johnny Mathis. I had held Mathis in very high esteem and wanted to emulate him.

Mr. Teevens remarked, "There already is a Johnny Mathis, and he does him better than you do."

Enough said.

I do have one suggestion for something to do when you don't have any money and you need to occupy yourself in a positive way. Take three old socks and a pound of black-eyed peas; divide the peas evenly three ways, filling the toes of the three socks. Sew the peas tightly into the toes and cut off the unfilled portion of the socks and teach yourself to juggle. This is one skill that you may never have to utilize in the context of a play; but you can learn it on your own, and I have rarely laughed more than when I was alone in my living room teaching myself this little trick.

Oh yes, and my approach, which I've never heard suggested in any of the manuals, is to stand facing the seat of a sofa or a double-wide chair. This helps to contain all those socks that you drop in the very beginning. You don't have to bend over so far to retrieve them.

## AUDITIONS

The single most important thing to have when walking into an audition is confidence! Particularly confidence that comes from knowing you are bringing your A game. You are the best you can be on that particular day.

Self-effacing ain't it? There was one singer on *American Idol* who sang like a bird but feigned shock every time she received a compliment. Simon finally called her on it because they had all seen enough. If you don't think you should be there, then what the hell are you doing there?

If, on audition day you have a cold, it doesn't matter unless the sickness is so bad that it keeps you from performing at or very near your best. I've always found that there is a stage in the early part of a cold when I feel like a singing superman—something about the way the sinuses are moistened or the way your head buzzes from the sound.

> **If you can't enter [the audition room] with confidence, you are better off staying home.**

If you can't enter with confidence, you are better off staying home. Going into an audition on a really off day will do you more harm than good. The people on the other side of the table don't want to hear about it. They just want you to walk in and be good, to be what they're looking for.

For all those productions where you audition and don't get the part, and you wonder why you didn't get it, it is important for you to know that when you audition for a whole table of people, it is quite rare for any one of those behind the table to be able to cast you without convincing a coalition of the others. Even if the director has set her sights on you as the only one capable of performing the role in question, she will have to sell that selection to at least one or two of the others. Rarely can a director make choices unilaterally.

However, it is often the case that several of the artistic staff will have a kind of veto power. Like lawyers during voir dire, each may have three or four uncontested refusals.

Few can say, "I *will* have that actor in this cast." More can say, "I will *not* have that actor in this cast."

This may seem like a fine distinction. I assure you it is not. For one off-Broadway show, I had done several workshops and had done well. The composer, the lyricist, the executive producer all wanted me for the title role. The director wanted someone else, or at least she didn't want me.

They had me audition for the role all over again, and even elongated the painful process by holding a callback. Remember, I had performed the role in readings and in workshop. The executive producer told me that he had wanted me, but he felt he had to let the director direct. It seems you can't count on anything.

## IN THE LONG RUN

I had done more than a hundred productions before I got to find out about life in the long-running show. Until I did *Les Misérables*, no job had lasted more than twenty weeks from the start of rehearsals until the last performance.

When I was in college, where a main-stage production ran for three consecutive weekends, I thought that no one should ever do a role for more than a year. It would have to get tiring by that point. There were performers for whom three weekends was too long a run.

I have since found that getting into a show is very like getting into the car for a trip. There is a kind of mental preparation that takes place. If you are getting into the car for a trip to the corner store, your brain prepares you for that length of trip, and I can get a bit upset if traffic makes it take three minutes longer than expected. However, if you are getting in to drive to the opposite coast, you make some snacks and settle in for the long haul.

When *Les Mis* had been running for a year, I didn't feel that I had gotten tired at all. Most of us were still taking guesses at how long the show would run. Five years seemed to be the going estimate. Most of us were settled in for quite a long ride—lots of snacks.

One aspect of *Les Mis* that made longevity easier was that performing it never ceased to be a challenge. We were, each of us in the ensemble, playing ten or twelve characters. We had to change costumes four or five times in the first eight minutes of the show. It couldn't get boring unless you were phoning it in, and how do you do that under those conditions?

The actors who couldn't cut it for a long run were the ones who put the onus on the show to entertain *them*. They were the ones who would stoop to playing pranks on one another, what in the Victorian era of the theater was called "guying."

## YOU CRACK ME UP (THOUGHTS ABOUT GUYING)

I don't think anyone has ever put much thought into how it began or who was the first; but my guess is that some unlikely thing happened to Agamemnon or Oedipus, and the entire cast broke into laughter, and somebody in the cast thought it would be a great idea to make the same thing happen at another performance. That's when guying was born.

In the nearly ten years that I performed in *Les Misérables*, there were a number of instances of people breaking because of random events. I remember several instances of Colm Wilkinson aiming his rifle in the air and pulling the trigger, expecting the loud report of a full charge of gunpowder only to hear the insignificant click of the rifle's hammer hitting an empty pan. He would turn back to us on the barricade, nod his head to signify that he had just dispatched Javert, and he'd mingle back in with the revolutionaries, muttering, "Would somebody please just throw in the rubber chicken?"

> "Would somebody please just throw in the rubber chicken?"

In one memorable instance, I was playing Enjolras (the revolutionary leader), and I ran up onto the barricade as I did every night, while the turntable was spinning to reveal the young Gavroche being picked off by sniper fire. After Gavroche had dutifully expired, our side of the playing area was brought back around into the view of the audience so that they could see our desolate reaction to this horrible loss. I was standing on the barricade, legs akimbo, facing downstage while the rest of the cast had their backs to the audience, looking to me for guidance. But when they looked to me, what they saw was not the inspirational leader of the revolt but poor old Joe with his pants split from belly button to spine. All those faces that were supposed to be looking up at me for inspiration were looking directly down at the stage floor with their shoulders bouncing.

If you've never tried it, singing while laughing is one of the hardest things in this world to do. For professionals it's nearly impossible. *Les Mis* has its lighter moments; but, for the most part, it's a serious story. Laughing through serious moments doesn't feel good. This is a difficult concept for many people to grasp. Because you're laughing, people think you are having a good time. And in some cases they will go to extraordinary measures to keep you laughing. I had one instance when I nearly had to clobber a dear friend to get him to stop.

In a highly visible moment in the show, I got the giggles. It was during "Empty Chairs at Empty Tables." This is Marius's big, sad ballad, when he acknowledges the loss of all of his friends from the ABC Café. All of us dead guys would line up at the back of the stage in darkness and do a slow, deadpan walk into the light just behind Marius. Simple, huh?

**Even in comedy, if the audience isn't in on the joke, it becomes sabotage.**

Well, my shoulders were bouncing, and every fiber of my being was trying to regain control. I was crying. I had flop sweat . . . the works. But one of my cohorts, standing right next to me, thought this was great! He did everything he could to keep me laughing. For the next week, in spite of all of my protests, he would do something to break my concentration at that very moment. The audience had no idea he was doing anything untoward; but to me it felt as if I was drowning, and instead of a floatation device, he was throwing me an anchor. That's guying.

In another moment of diversion, Javert, at the end of the barricade scene, looked down into the sewer grate only to be shot from below with a water pistol. That's also guying.

Here's my point of view on this. We are involved in live theater. Things happen. When it's done on purpose, it's unforgivable. Even in comedy, if the audience isn't in on the joke, it becomes sabotage. It is not contributing to the common good.

## LONG RUNS AND PRODUCTION CONTRACTS

When the show had been running for almost ten years and Cameron Mackintosh said that his *Les Misérables* was suffering from long-runitis, he could possibly have fixed the shortcomings that he saw by replacing two or three people. He wouldn't have gotten as much press as his entire restructuring garnered, but I thought he threw out quite a few hardworking babies with the bathwater.

I had a unique perspective on this whole series of events. The day everyone in the cast got their notices, I was playing the last performance of a limited-term contract. At that point I had left the show several times to do other things and had been hired back as a swing. I could go on, at a moment's notice, for any one of fourteen tracks in the show. I had gotten a good look at every performer onstage from a variety of vantage points. There were a few folks who, by that time, had figured out ways to phone it in.

But it was the way in which things were handled that created the controversy. A production contract, the mother contract for Actor's Equity Association upon which all of the other Equity contracts is based, is, in essence, an agreement about acceptable minimums: this is allowable, that is not. We will work for this amount of money. That amount is just too little, and none of us will work for that.

Very long runs of Broadway shows have presented some interesting circumstances that would have been difficult to litigate prior to their occurrence.

In the early eighties, Martin Charnin raised quite a ruckus in the theater industry by walking in one day after seeing a performance of *Annie* and summarily firing about half of the cast. He decided that the show was looking tired, and this was one way to fix it.

Hue and cry from the membership.

We can't allow this!

The next time production contracts were negotiated, the just cause clause was adopted. It became more difficult to fire actors under contract. Management had to show just cause. The actor had to be showing up late too frequently or refusing to take direction or any number of other things, and notice of the infractions had to be put in writing; but one couldn't just be let go at the whim of management without there being some kind of severance package commensurate with the length of time that a performer had been under contract.

Okay. So, fast forward to 1996. *Les Mis* has been running for just under ten years, and Sir Cameron Mackintosh decides that he's not going to approach *Les Mis*'s tenth anniversary with the show looking like this.

One week in September or October of that year, a notice was posted on the board of a "note session" after the Sunday matinee. Well, everyone knew that something was up. They *never* had note sessions on Sunday after the brunch show. The end of the Sunday show was the beginning of the day off.

Stage management was sworn to secrecy. No one was answering the myriad questions as to what this was about. The company was in a tizzy about what it could possibly be. Some had figured it out by the time Sunday came around; but no one knew exactly what was going to happen, and absolutely no one knew just *how* it would happen.

Here comes the Sunday matinee. Remember, actors have been performing all week with this unidentifiable weight hanging over their heads. I finished the final performance required of me for that contract, got out of costume, and packed my things.

By the time I was on my way out the stage door, all was becoming clear. The entirety of the cast had lined up—from the stage into the stage-right wing, into the hallway, and out the stage door onto Forty-sixth Street. Everyone, in turn, was given a sealed envelope with their name on the outside. Inside the envelope was one of three messages paraphrased here.

1. As of such and such a date, your services will no longer be required. Consider this notice of termination.
2. We would like you to audition for the artistic staff so that we can determine if we would like you to continue as a performer in this production.
3. We would like you to continue as a performer in this production.

So, for that number two statement, these actors were being asked to audition for the possibility of performing the role that they were currently playing in a Broadway show. I'm sure you can understand that a few of these folks just said, "No thanks." There is something demeaning about being asked to audition for the role that you are currently playing. There is a sense of proprietorship that goes along with performing a role, a sense of ownership. This sense was gravely shaken for some people; and their egos, or something, led them to refuse.

Some of these were surprised to find that refusing the audition was tantamount to quitting. They were walking away from the severance packages that had been required for those who had been dismissed outright. I know that at least one of those packages included more than thirty thousand pretax dollars. They wished someone had told them. When something like that happens, you need to somehow not let your emotions rule the day. If nothing else, you've got to carefully consider the wording of your contract.

## WORKING WITH DIRECTORS

Very few actors are ever in the position to choose the director for a project—I know I never have—so knowing the director with whom you're working becomes a matter of "forewarned is forearmed." In other words, any advance knowledge you can gain about a director will allow you to prepare for those idiosyncrasies over which you have absolutely no control. I mean, you can choose to not accept a contract; but unless the pay is totally crap, that's usually a matter of cutting off your nose to spite your face.

I look at the actor's job as a variation of connecting the dots. The dots are usually first set up by the playwright. The words on the page give us our framework. It is up to the actor to connect those dots. But the director is he who must be trusted to guide the production to a sense of unity and a clear telling of the story. The director will introduce her own set of dots.

Some directors set their dots very far apart. It's almost as if, once the casting is complete, their job with the actors is finished and they can spend their time concentrating on production values. I found this to be the case with Wilford Leach, who directed *The Human Comedy*. The only direction that I remember getting from Mr. Leach was about adjusting my stance so that I was open to more of the audience. Early on in rehearsal, I'd asked which entrance I should use to get into the playing area to begin a scene with Donnie Kehr. Wilford just said, "Well, which entrance would you use?" I picked one, and we were on our way.

The other end of the spectrum is a director who wants to personally choreograph every movement of the last digit of your pinkie. If you've ever heard the term "an actor's director," this is not one of those. This director must dictate every aspect, and the actor's job becomes one of imitating whatever the director sees as necessary to her telling of the story.

Most directors fall somewhere in between these two extremes, but good or bad can run the full gamut. It is generally much more difficult to please the more choreographic directors. They tend to come

## CONNECTING THE DOTS

- The actor's job is a variation of connecting the dots.
- The dots are usually first set up by the playwright.
- The words on the page give us our framework. It is up to the actor to connect those dots.
- The director will introduce her own set of dots.
- Some directors set their dots very far apart. It's almost as if, once the casting is complete, their job with the actors is finished and they can spend their time concentrating on production values.

For more go to http://www.nowyoutellmebooks.com/actors

in with a detailed vision of the finished product; and you, as the actor, must contribute to the fulfillment of that vision.

The directors toward the other end of the spectrum can be difficult in that it is often a challenge to get them to say anything direct. You have to go with the approach that "if she's not saying anything, I must be doing it right."

I'm happy to report that I have never worked with one of those mega-lomaniacs with the riding crop and a patch over one eye who scream every direction at you as if you are completely stupid. I don't doubt that they exist, but I seem to have escaped them.

I have dealt with a few whom I thought had been promoted to a position several levels beyond their competence.

The clearest case of this involved an amazingly important personage in the world of Broadway musicals: Alan Jay Lerner. Yes, he wrote a few of the greatest musicals in the history of the theater; but what he really wanted to do was direct.

Around 1980, Alan Jay Lerner directed a revival of *My Fair Lady* in London. It was very well received. Lerner felt that this qualified him to direct the new show that he was writing with Charles Strouse called *Dance a Little Closer*. It came to be known as *Close a Little Faster*.

In the London revival of *My Fair Lady*, Lerner simply had to remount what had been very ably staged in the original by Moss Hart. No lightweight there. But with *Dance a Little Closer* it was all new. The staging had never been created for Lerner to re-create. He didn't seem to have a clue. For the most part, the actors had to figure it out for themselves.

Lerner couldn't explain what he wanted, he could only demonstrate. And his demonstrations were always one of two possibilities. To wit: he would either feign the casualness of a Rat Pack mobster with a cigarette dangling from his lip or channel Stanley Kowalski screaming "Stella!" There was nothing in between.

Approach a difficult director the same way you approach working with any other. Aim for the center of your character and commit yourself to the fulfillment of your role. I actually remember a wonderful actor by the name of

I. M. Hobson using military terms such as "entrenchment." He and his acting partner in *Dance a Little Closer* were "entrenching themselves" in their characters because they were afraid that Mr. Lerner might try to suggest something.

If you keep going for the center and I hope that you understand that I'm not suggesting every character exists somewhere in the middle of the road; if the center of your character is somewhere on the fringes of sanity, that is the center that you must strive for and the director never finds anything acceptable in what you are doing, then you have simply come up against a wall. Turn away from the wall.

The wall to which I'm referring is a kind of dark epiphany moment when I thought I had really understood what a director was looking for only to find, very late in the game, that we weren't on the same page at all.

The clearest example of this not working was a production of *Dames at Sea* that I did up at the Helen Hayes in Nyack. We had been rehearsing for more than three weeks with the director saying that everything that I was doing was really good. Then as we went into technical rehearsals, with a live audience just two or three days away, he says, "Could you just make it all funnier?"

Wall!

He had been laughing all during rehearsals. Everything, from my perspective, had been going very well. Suddenly, he's giving me the much-parodied direction to make it funnier? That's just the worst thing that a director can say to an actor. If you ask for funny when the impression for three weeks is that it already is funny, it's tantamount to saying that he's been lying to you throughout the rehearsal process and nothing that you've done up to that point is any good at all.

We actually ended up standing on the stage and discussing this for an extended period of time. The other actors went back to their dressing rooms to await the final outcome.

What I ended up doing was to try very hard to forget that the discussion had ever happened. I focused on the direction that I had been given earlier in the rehearsal process, and I played it based upon that direction. That was how I chose to turn away from the wall.

There is no way that I could have walked away from the production. There were no understudies. There was no Eve waiting in the wings fully prepared to go on for me. I had to continue.

For the very same reasons, the director couldn't, at that late hour, just tell me that I was fired. The production needed me.

This is the one instance in the thirty years that I have been pursuing theatrical employment in New York when I was unable to find common ground with a director.

If you must, you can do that. It's never easy. It's kind of like divorce. Even when people say it was amicable, it can't really have been amicable. But it can be done. It may come down to a matter of making the case that "if that's what you want me to do, you picked the wrong person." Now, how do we move on from here?

As long as you are involved in a production, the negotiation never fully ends.

You may not know that there is a probation period of five days written into the production contract. If you have gone all the way through the audition process and are cast in a Broadway show, the producers still have the first five days of rehearsal to discover that they have made a mistake. I have never seen this option taken, but it does exist.

What I have seen is a couple of instances when an actor has been engaged and goes through the rehearsal process and is *then* sent home. Now, this actor has a pretty firm bit of paperwork on which to stand. The producers can't stop paying him. They can take his name out of the program and not allow him to play the role; but they have to pay him through the term of his contract or through the final performance, whichever comes first. They also have to pay the person that they've brought in to replace him.

You can understand that this is not a path easily chosen by a producer.

## WORKING WITH ACTORS

There are actors who are not collaborative. Be prepared for facing the occasional actor who truly cares only for himself. The rest of the production matters not a wit. Ladies and gentlemen, meet a man I'll call Mr. Broadway Star.

Here's the thing: He's good. Very good. But you don't want to work with him, because you don't work *with* him. You work and he works, but you do not work together.

Here's a for instance.

Pat Cook and Rick Freyer had written a wonderful musical adaptation of *Captains Courageous*. It had been read by a couple of casts, and it had been work-shopped and done in full production at Ford's Theatre in Washington, D.C.

Now, Manhattan Theatre Club was going to workshop it again with the idea of eventually doing it in one of their spaces at City Center.

They got Mr. Broadway Star to play Manuel, the Portuguese fisherman.

This is a play about men working together to wrestle a living from the sea. Shipmates and dory mates and camaraderie and sharing are what this story is all about. Apparently, Lynne Meadow, our director, thought Mr. Star was a good fit.

From day one he set himself apart. Where one would expect that the point of rehearsals would be to build a sense of oneness within this ensemble, we had an ensemble and Mr. Star.

In the context of group scenes, which was a significant portion of the play, a scene would build momentum and intensity and a rhythm, and then it was time for him to speak. Blink, blink. He would wait . . . blink . . . until all eyes had turned to him and would deliver his lines as if he were in an entirely different play that was just starting every time he had to speak. Unconscionable.

He worked out his through-line entirely on his own. Do you remember those trust exercises you do in Acting 101? Him, not so much.

We got to the point of performing our rehearsal-room staging for industry people early one weekday afternoon. The audience was made up of agents and producers and a few friends, most of whom had left the office with the intention of being away for a couple of hours and then returning to finish off their workday.

Our show started off with a short scene in which Harvey Cheyne establishes his regrettable character and then falls off of an ocean liner over the Grand Banks. The scene shifts to the deck of the fishing schooner where most of the action of the show takes place: a big number with lots of props, including numerous ropes and halyards, which required five to ten minutes to preset for each run-through. Big finish to the number, and things go quiet for the entrance of Manuel in his fishing dory. And here comes Mr. Star.

And he stops.

This is paraphrased, but he said something to the effect of "I'm very nervous. Could we just take it back so I can get started again?"

The cast all look to stage management, and to our director, to see just what we should do. We get a nod, and we all begin setting up for the end of the big number that we have just finished and cleared from the stage. We pick up with the last chorus of the big number, and the audience very graciously applauds our second effort at this rousing sea chantey; and things go quiet for the entrance of Manuel in his fishing dory, and here comes Mr. Star.

And he stops.

Paraphrasing again, "No, what I meant was, could we go back from the beginning?"

I had heard stories in which he stopped the orchestra in concert when he hadn't gotten a song started just the way he wanted. Reports were that someone from the audience had gotten fed up and had screamed something like "JUST SING THE F---ING SONG!!!!" We were not blessed with anyone of such noble character in our afternoon of theater.

We looked to our director. She indicated that, yes, we should go back to the beginning. We all, except Mr. Star, helped to reestablish the preset of all of those ropes and buckets. All of the cast rewound their characters to the top of the show, never mind that they had all been very capable of being ready to begin at the appointed time. We would all find our way back to the beginning of our journey, back to the start of the yellow brick road, and hope that this time he would find that the preparation had been satisfactory to him.

A few of the audience left.

They had allowed X amount of time away from their desks. They knew that they wouldn't make it back that quickly, and they'd seen enough.

Those who stayed amazingly rewarded our *third* big finish to the opening number with a round of applause that I could not have mustered. And finally, this time, the show carried on.

Manhattan Theatre Club did go on to do a full production of *Captains Courageous* at City Center. I wasn't available to reprise my role, but the show turned out to be quite terrific. A different actor, Treat Williams, played Manuel. He was great!

## MAKING A LIFE

### FOCUS ON THE CENTER

Here's an idea that I embraced soon after arriving in New York and that continues to have a strong influence on my life on- and offstage. Moss Hart was the speaker, and he was speaking to our friend Alan Jay Lerner. He said, "Stop trying to be different. You don't have to be different to be good. To be good is different enough."

**"You don't have to be different to be good. To be good is different enough."**

Usually, great ideas for ticks or mannerisms come off as false and unsupported. See Jim Carrey. Obviously, I'm not saying that you can't be successful if you practice bad acting. I just don't like it.

Go for the center. Your uniqueness can't help but make everything you do different from anything that has ever been done before.

## CONTINUING EDUCATION

For this actor, the idea of actively improving one's craft is fraught with dangers in that it can easily lead to change for change's sake. That being said, there are certainly basic skills that can be honed and polished.

The best pitchers in the major league all have coaches that help keep them from developing bad habits. (Even Tiger Woods has a swing coach.) We can all benefit from an objective eye.

I was working on my sixth Broadway production when the need for a good voice teacher became very apparent to me. I had had teachers in the past, but I hadn't studied in four or five years. I was a professional. I knew what I was doing. I was performing *Les Misérables* eight times a week.

That's exactly when it can creep up on you.

I was singing through sickness. Or all the *Les Mis* stage smoke was getting to me, or I was developing some tensions that I wasn't aware of, or all of the above.

Who knows? The point is that things were happening in my singing that I didn't have control over. I needed an objective eye, someone I could trust to observe what I was doing and to help me clean it up. The doctor who did my surgery, cutting that polyp off my vocal chord, directed me to the voice teacher who saved me for the rest of my career. Joan Lader helped me to rediscover freedom in singing. She helped me to rediscover *my* voice. Remember that mentor thing.

We all continue to develop. We may increase our awareness. We may work at developing sensitivity and perception. I think that the best teachers of acting help us to avoid the pitfalls, remind us that less is more, point out where we may exhibit excess or timidity. The rest is all about exposure.

Exposing ourselves to all aspects of life will serve to increase our acting vocabulary. We will continue to say many of the same things, but we will deepen the nuance with every step we take. It is never wasted. Life may be wasteful in other ways, but life's experience is food for acting that never rots.

## DON'T JUST DO IT

"It's a harsh business. There's no room for Mr. Nice Guy."

This absolutely is not the case. The vast majority of the people whom I've come across in the theater have been delightful, good-natured, talented folks who just happen to be in a business under a public microscope.

We are in a business in which one often hears about people being mean or catty to one another. The reality shows on television play up this idea and get great ratings for their efforts. It's easy to see how Joe Public could come away with the perception that everyone climbs all over whomever gets in his or her way.

I must admit that when I came to New York, I was expecting everyone to have a pretty thick crust. I had also been warned about the no-nonsense approach to the study of acting. Every teacher was a ballbuster. Be ready for the whipping of your life.

I had the good fortune to be invited to take a master class with Sanford Meisner, a madman who still smoked despite having had his larynx removed because of cancer. I had been led to expect an emotional brute who would rend your psyche and reduce every actor to an emotional ash heap. It's not true.

He was serious. He was amazingly succinct. He had lost his voice box and had to laboriously burp his words when lecturing. But it seemed that this had created a circumstance in which nothing was wasted. It took him so long to make a statement that he chose his words very carefully. It was easy to keep up with him if you were taking notes, and we did.

He did seem to be able to tap into people's emotional hang-ups: girls with father issues and guys with Oedipus troubles. But his strongest ability was his eye for honesty. Don't try and fake out Sanford Meisner. He'll get you.

Isn't that exactly what you would wish for in an acting teacher?

The whole point of his repetition exercise was to eliminate all of the extraneous stuff and make you focus on what was there. Then elements would be added: an activity, urgency, intention, an event just outside the room, a knock on the door.

Each of these elements had to have importance to the actor. Nothing would work if there wasn't some kind of strong emotional connection, importance. If the exercise didn't work, Mr. Meisner would ask, "What were you doing?"

If the word *just* fell anywhere in the explanation, Mr. Meisner would quip, "It wasn't important enough." If you were "just" doing anything, it wasn't important enough. You would have to try again next class, and do a preparation that had importance for you.

"Don't just do something; stand there." That's what all this is leading to. That's my favorite Sanford Meisner line. If you are *just* doing this or that, who cares? You don't care enough about it; how is an audience going to care?

## MOMENTS OF ABSOLUTE ECSTASY

No one ever told me that it could be perfect, that there could be moments of absolute ecstasy.

I was told about some of the pitfalls. I was warned that the life of an actor would be difficult. I was taught much about preparing. I think it was my aunt Eileen who dutifully warned me that I would have to step on a lot of people to be successful. (That's not true, Aunt Eileen.)

But what do you do when it's perfect?

Tom O'Horgan and John Mauceri set up my moment of perfection. John remembered my audition for a production of Strauss's *Wiener Blut* at the Washington National Opera—although he couldn't remember my name. He called Frank Rizzo and asked for "that Polish kid." Thankfully, Frank Rizzo did remember, "Oh yeah, that's Joe Kolinski."

At the time, I'm playing Perchik in *Fiddler on the Roof* at the Darien Dinner Theater. I get a call on the backstage pay phone from my agent about auditioning for Leonard Bernstein's *Mass*. Sure, I'm familiar; I saw David Cryer play the Celebrant in Detroit in '75.

I sing "A Simple Song" and "*Gloria Tibi*" for Mauceri and O'Horgan, and they tell me I'm it.

Several days later my agent calls. "They're saying that Lenny [Leonard Bernstein] is feeling left out of the process. Bring a pianist and all of your audition stuff over to the Dakota so he can hear you."

I bring my buddy, composer Skip Kennon, to play for me.

We're shown into the room that overlooks the corner of Seventy-third and Central Park West. Lenny makes his entrance, smoking. He's so much shorter than I had expected.

I sang almost everything in my book. Almost all of it was his: *Candide*, Tony in *West Side Story*, "A Simple Song," "*Gloria Tibi*." He coaches me through half of the songs. He shows me how to make the most of the triplets. He wants me to smoke with him, and I do.

I don't remember leaving the apartment. I remember being in that elevator from the era of *Time and Again* and stepping out into the spot on Seventy-second Street where John Lennon had been taken from us only a few months before.

Lenny had approved my appointment.

Perfection is something that can only be appreciated after the fact.

My wedding day was perfect.

The moment of my daughter's birth was perfect.

That time with Lenny was perfect.

What do you do when it's perfect?

Fill your cup.

And make your garden grow. ★

For more from Joseph go to
http://www.nowyoutellmebooks.com/actors.

# BRENDA STRONG

## "A successful acting career is really about relationships."

B renda Strong is one of Hollywood's most prolific actresses. Perhaps best known as Ann Ewing in the reboot of *Dallas* and Mary Alice in *Desperate Housewives*, she has appeared in over 100 television series from *Twin Peaks* and *Seinfeld* to *The Closer* and *Curb Your Enthusiasm*. Her favorite film roles include Ellen in *The Deep End of the Ocean* and Melanie in *Black Dog*. She can also sing and dance.

# MAKING A LIVING

## GETTING STARTED IN L.A.

I got my degree in Musical Theater from Arizona State University in 1983, and I headed for New York because that's where it seemed musical theater people should be. I stayed with a friend who was in a Broadway show and I did some summer stock auditions. But I didn't feel like I was a good candidate for chorus because of my height—I was too tall to fit in. And I noticed that the headliners on Broadway were from television and film—they weren't Broadway actors; they were celebrities.

So I decided to go to Los Angeles. I'm from a very small town in the Pacific Northwest, and I didn't feel emotionally prepared to handle the intensity of New York. I felt far removed from any kind of support system there, and in L.A., on the West Coast, I would be closer to my family. My plan was to build a name for myself and then go back and do the types of theater roles that I wanted to do. At least that was a way for me to make sense of the choice. I was trained in musical theater and light opera and, to this day, I would still like to go back and do Broadway. I have absolute faith that will be a part of my future. I'm working towards that now.

I moved to Orange County, California, because I was offered a place to stay, rent-free, with the mother of my boyfriend at the time. Also, Orange County is far enough out of L.A. that I felt safe—it was close, but not too close. I was definitely a small town girl, and it took me a while to adjust to living in a big city.

My dream was to do high quality *anything* as an actor. Ironically, I ended up doing a play when I got to L.A. because that's what I knew. It was a one-man show with Doug Warhit in which there was a fantasy sequence and I was the fantasy. A casting director in the audience saw me. She needed a French-speaking, Las Vegas showgirl type for a film she was casting and asked if I did accents. I said, "Yes, of course." She brought me in and I actually booked the film! That kind of thing never happens to actors, that I got an audition and a job without having an agent.

I needed to get an agent to negotiate the deal. It was the standard Scale Plus Ten but still, I needed someone. I had a friend who was willing to introduce me to his agent, who negotiated the deal. He ended up being my agent for about a year and a half, until I had the wherewithal to get a manager. That manager introduced me to a better agent, one who could be more effective for where I was and what I wanted. Two of the agents within that agency then became managers, and ended up getting me another agency. It's been an evolution.

A successful acting career is really about relationships—about the people you know who know others. Had I been more adept as a younger artist, I would have waited for a better agent. I was so happy that anyone wanted me that I went with an agency that couldn't get me the types of roles that I was right for—and prepared for. So I ended up with a mid-range television agent, as opposed to a higher-end agent who could package me, and put me in television projects and feature films. It took me longer to climb up through the ranks that way.

But the truth is, you never know how your career is going to start. You make choices based on what's available. And you never know how people will be influential in your life. Junie Lowry-Johnson was the casting director sitting in the audience who gave me my first job. Years later she cast me in a television movie with Kenny Rogers in which I worked with her two brothers, one of whom is a director, and the other, a film producer. That led to her casting me in *Star Trek: The Next Generation* and, years later, in *Desperate Housewives*. She has been pivotal in the shape of my career. I owe her a tremendous amount.

## COLD-READINGS

I ended up taking a few cold-reading classes because the first audition I went to was with [casting director] Simon Ayer, and he told my agent that

I didn't know how to cold-read. Actually, what I think he said was, "She doesn't know how to act," which is different. But I didn't take it personally: I took it as a challenge. I realized that auditioning for film and television required a different muscle. I'd had theatrical training, which emphasizes building roles from the ground up. So I had to reeducate myself because I was on the wrong coast for the education I got. I realized that I had a big learning curve ahead of me.

I didn't have the money to pay for the classes, so I made a deal to clean my acting teacher's house in exchange. I was working three jobs; one as a housecleaner, another as an aerobics instructor at the Richard Simmons Anatomy Asylum, and yet another in skin care at I. Magnin in La Prairie in Orange County.

The only thing about the cold-reading class that was an "Aha!" moment for me was when I realized that I was a lot better than I thought I was. Part of that realization came from having to make strong choices very quickly when cold-reading, which can also be very dangerous, because then you can't get to the depths. You might be able to make strong superficial choices but, unless you do the backstory work, you also run the risk of getting lazy. For me, it was learning how to trust myself enough to know that I didn't *have* to do a three-month rehearsal in order to be ready to go on. I could do a three-minute rehearsal or a thirty-minute rehearsal, and be ready to be present and shaped. The biggest lesson was learning to trust myself more.

One thing I did right was that I knew who I was. I cared deeply about the craft, and I brought that respect to everything that I did. I cared. I wasn't a lazy actor. I didn't take anything for granted, and I worked really hard. I was professional and I showed up—that's what I did right.

What I did wrong was that I thought there was a certain way I had to *be* in order to be successful. It took me awhile to find my authentic assets—to know how to make the role fit me, as opposed to me trying to fit the role. When that perspective shifted, I started becoming more successful. When I didn't think that there was a certain way that I had to be to fit the role—but that, instead, there was a way for me to actually see myself in the role and to express that uniqueness—*that* was when things started shifting for me.

And, truthfully, it didn't happen that long ago—probably about ten years ago.

## FINDING THE TIME TO FIND SUCCESS

I got my SAG [Screen Actors Guild] card in 1985, at which time I was still teaching aerobics and doing the I. Magnin skin care job. I was working twelve-hour days. I would go to I. Magnin at 9:00 in the morning and, if I had an audition, I would leave Orange County to drive to L.A., do the audition, drive back to Orange County, and work until they closed at 9:00 at night. My manager believed in me so much that she was willing to adjust her schedule around me, which was amazing. And I still managed to be the top seller on my floor at I. Magnin.

But the problem was that I had no life force left. I was burning the candle at both ends, and at a certain point, my fiancée said, "If you are serious about acting, you need to focus on it full-time." He gave me his blessing to quit working for a year so I could focus on auditioning and my craft. It allowed me to take a [Sanford] Meisner course that had a more intense time commitment. It allowed me to focus, and I started booking a lot more jobs.

I never had to work another job besides acting after that—primarily because of commercials, not theatrical jobs. I was working enough commercials that I was able to support myself and, eventually, to support the family. I went from feeling that I was the inconsistent, crazy artist that needed somebody who was stable to becoming the stable one. That was a huge leap for me. I never imagined that I would be in a financial position to support others beside myself.

## MANAGING MONEY

I was horribly trained with money. My parents were land rich and cash poor. We never had extra money. I grew up shopping at Goodwill. I had lived "without" for such a long time, so I never felt like I had to have a certain amount of *things*. And I certainly knew how to stretch a dollar! What I didn't know was how to manage one.

You never know how much you're going to make as an actor when you're not on a series and don't have a consistent income. It's hard to budget yourself, because you don't know what the budget is. I realized that there wasn't a choice: I couldn't just say I wasn't good with money—I had to get good. I had the erroneous idea that safety equals money and that money equals safety. I've come to find out since that this is not true, actually; your sense of being safe in the world has to

> **Your sense of being safe in the world has to do with who you are and not what you have.**

do with who you are and not what you have. I learned this the hard way. So my philosophy became when there was a lot of money coming in, pretend that there *wasn't*. Always put money aside.

Always give money away, too. For me, if I made one hundred dollars, I'd want to give ten dollars of it away because money is energy. If I tried to hold onto it and clutch it, it would get stagnant. I had to find some way to generate a sense of flow and of gratitude. So even when money was tight, I always felt that if I could give something away, more would come in since I was being generous with it. I wasn't irresponsible—I wasn't giving away money that I needed to eat or live on—but it gave me a sense of generosity of spirit that allowed me to feel like there was more coming.

During the Depression, my dad's family had a farm. They ended up feeding a lot of people who otherwise wouldn't have eaten. My mom always donated her time to the Indian reservation and education. So there was always a sense of generosity in my upbringing, of giving to those who were less privileged. It makes you feel connected and good; it has served me very well.

## AUDITIONING THE AUDITIONERS

I used to go into auditions thinking, "I hope they like me." Now, I go in thinking, "I hope I like them." As I have become more seasoned, I use the audition now to gauge whether I want to work with the people in the room. It's about trying to connect my energy with the energy in the room to see if a collaboration is possible, if we can have a conversation where we're on the same page. It's important for young actors to know that not only are they auditioning you, you're auditioning them. It's also helpful to remember that everybody has fear. Having fear doesn't mean that there is something wrong; it's a healthy measure of the human condition. And you're not the only person in the room who is afraid—they're afraid that they're not going to find the right person. Their biggest hope is that *you're* that person.

> I used to go into auditions thinking, "I hope they like me." Now, I go in thinking, "I hope I like them."

Knowing that they're on your side when you walk in, knowing they hope you're going to be the answer, allows you to relax a little bit. There is no wrong way to audition as long as you're true to yourself. Either you're what they're looking for or you aren't. As long as you're on your own instrument, there is no "wrong." What will happen is that they'll see you and they'll think, "Well, she's not right for this, but she'd be damn good for this over here."

Of course not passing out is always good. But seriously, I don't know that anybody does a good audition, because it's a very inorganic process with little relationship to the work itself. The good news is that it's a level playing field and everybody is in the same boat.

## CRITERIA FOR TAKING ROLES

As a younger actor you don't have the luxury of turning down roles. You're just trying to get work, and you're happy when you get a role. It's not about shaping a career; it's about surviving—as in, putting food on the table. I only started feeling like I had the ability to turn down roles when my basic needs were met, which only happened about seven years ago when I was cast on *Desperate Housewives*. That's when I started to experience having a regular role and a regular paycheck. Then I had the opportunity to say, "No, that's a role that I've done before, and it's not going to put my career on any kind of new trajectory." I was able to say "No" because, at that point, it wasn't about the money anymore. It was about doing something that added value to me as a human being and intrigued me as an artist.

> I remember a critic saying something like, "What is a good actress like you doing in a bad sitcom like this?" Um, paying the mortgage.

Unfortunately there haven't been that many things that have met those criteria. Sometimes it's about paying for your kid's education, so a lot of choices are still made out of necessity. And the bad movie of the week isn't something that you've necessarily chosen to do, either, but you still get raked over the coals for doing it! I remember a critic saying something like, "What is a good actress like you doing in a bad sitcom like this?" Um, paying the mortgage. That's the reality of the choices that need to be made.

## DEALING WITH A BAD DIRECTOR

Working with a good director is play; working with a bad director is work. You have to try to interpret what it is that they want. Some directors make observations, but they don't really direct. You have to know what *you* want and be clear about that inside yourself: do all your work beforehand and know what you want out of the scene because, at least then you'll have some structure to work from.

My definition of a bad director is someone who gets in the way of your creativity and your progress as an actor. I'll never forget one director, specifically. My initial instinct was that this guy was either a genius or he was insane. Turned out to be pretty much the latter. He was over-directing the actors so that they didn't even have a chance to breathe in the scene. As the shoot progressed, he was starting to give line readings and was even trying to direct which way we would look when we said a line.

I finally took the bull by the horns and told him to give us a couple of runs at a scene, and then come back and talk to us. "Just let us breathe the scene, let us show you what we can do, and then let's talk. You're over-directing before we've even had a chance to discover how to relate to each other. If it's not what you want, then come back and tell us."

Afterward, one of the younger actors came up and thanked me, because we hadn't had a chance to get anything of quality done. That's the only time I've told a director to back off and let us do our work! If I had respected him I wouldn't have said anything, but I'd totally lost respect for him by that point.

On stage, the actors are the leaders because the actors and the audience shape the experience. In film, the director is the leader because he has a vision that is greater than your particular part in that vision. Sometimes you can fight for something you think is right, but if it's not within the realm of his vision, you can end up working against yourself. It's important to know how to be a good leader and a good follower and to recognize that there is a time and place for both.

Ideally you and the director learn to trust each other, and it's great when you get the opportunity to work with people who trust themselves, too. That is rare, especially in television, where the directors don't really

**A good performance is like a good wine that starts to breathe and to open up and all the different notes get richer.**

direct anymore. Instead they point their cameras and let the actors who know their characters do their work for them. But if you and your director trust each other, he or she will let you do your work, and then they add nuance and shape. This allows you to go deeper and be more specific and more interesting. A good performance is like a good wine that starts to breathe and to open up and all the different notes get richer.

## GOOD WRITING

I find that I can memorize good writing instantly, but bad writing takes me forever because it's inorganic. It's not well constructed and it doesn't make sense in my body or in my mind. I'll edit bad writing without even being aware that I'm doing it—I'll leave certain sentences out. I was working with Quentin Tarantino, and I kept leaving a section of a speech out. He finally thanked me and said that I was right, that the section shouldn't have been there. In that case, I left it out because it interrupted the natural rhythm of the scene. Tarantino was incredibly flexible about using the audition process as another level of his own creativity. That kind of collaboration is fun.

## PRO ACTORS ARE PROACTIVE

Proactive actors are the ones people remember. They're the ones who don't just show up, do the job, and go home, but the ones who actually cultivate relationships. "Thank you" notes are always appreciated. Even when you don't get the role, write a note telling them that you hope it goes well and that you hope to work with them in the future.

Taking the time to show people that you care, and that you are thinking about them, often paves the way for the next thing. This relationship-building business is exactly that: every new relationship is built on previous ones. Practice cultivating relationships with people who are your tribe, people you like working with. I did a play recently called *Titus Redux,* which is based on *Titus Andronicus,* and invited people with whom I'd cultivated relationships to come see it. Many of them talked about how they had no idea I could do Shakespeare and that I could move like that. Keep people engaged in what you are doing in a way that allows them to feel connected. Whether it's making phone calls, scheduling a lunch, or writing a quick letter, these links help generate interest in what you're up to.

Another way to be proactive is by being creative. I'm developing a project right now with a friend because the subject matter interests me. Because of the creative collaboration, and because there's so much juicy energy flowing, I want to reach out to other people in order to make the project a reality. When people start to see that you care about the creative process and you're actively doing things, not just waiting for people to give you jobs, it elevates their respect for you.

It also doesn't hurt to put yourself on tape saying that you would like to be considered for a part, that you'd really like to be seen for this. Yes, there's certain protocol you need to follow in the industry. But there are many stories of actors who have campaigned for roles, gotten them—and delivered. They proved that they were the right person for the role. The ultimate goal is to join the company of the Ben Afflecks and Matt Damons of the world who generate their own careers. People want to work with them because that creative energy is appealing and addictive and it keeps you alive and vibrant.

Don't be desperate. Be an advocate for your career. Be proactive. Don't sit and wait for people to give you roles. Generate work.

There was a role in the film *The Deep End of the Ocean* that I really wanted to play. My agent had tried everything to get me an audition, but they weren't interested in seeing me because Michelle Pfeiffer had been cast in the lead and they felt that Michelle and I wouldn't be good friends. My agent told them that they were absolutely wrong and asked to just get me into the audition room.

I knew it was one of those circumstances where they didn't want me. I knew that every ounce of my creativity and ingenuity would be needed when I walked in that door.

The character I wanted to play was a woman who came to the rescue of her best friend under very difficult circumstances. Then, under intense pressure, she continued on to find this child who had been abducted. She becomes the emotional anchor. I thought, "How can I possibly reveal that in a simple audition?"

Here's what happened.

At the time my agent got me the audition, my mother had a stroke and I had flown back East to see her where she was staying with my sister. Suddenly the audition came through out of nowhere and I had to fly back early—only to find out that my car had been stolen! I had to call the police, file a report, and figure out how to get to the audition on time. By the time I walked into that room, I felt like I was already embodying the character who was dealing with one disaster after another and having to organize all these things with presence of mind and hold it all together. I told them the story of my last forty-eight hours. I think the director immediately thought, "Okay, that's our girl."

> **Everything is a gift, even the traffic accident before you get there, or being late, or the fight you had with your boyfriend, or the cat throwing up on your shoes, or whatever it is. Everything is an opportunity to be fuller when you walk into that room. Life will work *for* you, if you understand that.**

Life has afforded me those opportunities organically. If I had said, "Oh my God, my mom shouldn't be having a stroke, and my car is stolen, and I'm never going to get this!" I could have used all those circumstances against myself. Instead, it turned out that it was just what I needed to walk into that room.

Being proactive is really about how you look at your life more than anything. Everything is a gift, even the traffic accident before you get there, or being late, or the fight you had with your boyfriend, or the cat throwing up on your shoes, or whatever it is. Everything is an opportunity to be fuller when you walk into that room. Life will work *for* you, if you understand that.

## ADVICE TO A YOUNG ACTOR

I told my son Zak [Henri] early on, "If you want to act, you have to train. You have to know your craft. I'm not getting you any meetings with any agents until you absolutely trust your instrument." And so he studied for three years with a really top-notch acting coach. I wanted him to have confidence in his ability before he felt he had to put the pedal to the metal and test himself. I wanted him to have the freedom to enjoy the process and not have the pressure.

It's hard to have the pressure of getting work before you've had the chance to explore and play and know your craft. The industry is different now than when I was starting out; it's much more difficult because agents don't take on the role of developing talent anymore. They're just fielding phone calls. They want the talent to do the work. The business is much more run by money than by belief in someone's talent.

This summer, Zak had a small part in a sweet film called *Teacher of the Year*. He was part of an ensemble and had four scenes where he had a line. I took him to dinner the night before and asked him what he wanted to get out of it, and he said, "Mom, it's just four lines." And I said, "Zak, every time you step on a set you have an opportunity to influence how everyone sees you. If you see yourself as an actor with only four lines, that's how everyone else is going to see you." I asked him whose career he admired and wanted to emulate, and he said Leonardo DiCaprio, Johnny Depp, George Clooney. I said, "If there was a young Leonardo DiCaprio or a young Johnny Depp or a young George Clooney stepping onto that set, how would he behave? Would he behave like he only had four lines and he wasn't that important and wouldn't get much out of it? Or would he show up thinking, 'I have a future that I'm living into, and I want all of you to become the ambassadors for that future.' So when you meet the costumer, when you sit in the makeup chair, when you talk to the assistant director, you are that future. You are already that person. You want them to be spreading the word, 'Oh my gosh, I just met this amazing kid who's going to be the next Leonardo DiCaprio.' But you have to embody that before you even step onto the set."

It's about learning to hold your future in your hands *now*, not thinking that someday you'll be there. Be that person now. Value yourself even though you don't have the experience to step into those shoes.

I also told Zak that if he ever thought of himself as more important than anyone or anything else on a set, that would be the end of it. That kind of entitlement and disrespect for other people's roles does not fly with me. As his parent, if he started to get a big head or he started to act important, I would pull him out of that world immediately. I've seen a lot of younger actors who think that the world revolves around them and that everybody should cater to them. Then they end up becoming arrested-development adults because they don't know how to be responsible for themselves. That was an important lesson that I wanted him to learn right away, that he wasn't more important than anyone else: he may be valuable, which is absolutely true—but not more important.

# MAKING A LIFE

## ACTING AND RELATIONSHIPS

Back when I was in college, I had dinner with the person with whom I was in love. It was very romantic. Then he said, "Look, Brenda, I want to marry you. But I don't want to marry an actress." And in that moment it became clear that this was not the right person for me. You can't separate the two—it's not like I'm choosing to do this!—it's who I am, so, good-bye!

From that moment I knew that I could only have someone in my life who believed and supported what I did. I was very fortunate in that I ended up marrying someone who really believed in me. In fact, he sometimes held belief in me when I didn't have belief in myself. I'm really grateful to have found that kind of true partner.

Also, I chose to get married in my twenties because I didn't like the attention that I was getting as a woman in the industry. I was often unsure if people hired me because they wanted to sleep with me, or if they hired me because I was the best person for the job. That sexual pressure is hard for a young actress to navigate. It was much easier for me to be married than to be single. I was happy to take that question right off the table.

It's sad to say, but when you have a dream and you're hungry to achieve that dream, people will take advantage of you if they can and if you let them. That's when you must have very firm boundaries. You have to become a savvy judge of character to know who has your best interests at heart and who doesn't. The more I valued my own self-worth and held my own power and said "No" to the things that made me uncomfortable, the better off I was.

Part of the deal with being an actor, with being somebody that people want to watch, is that there is a certain necessary level of charisma and natural magnetism. And there are some people who will prey on that quality and want to either possess the person who has it or have it for themselves. And that is why you have agents and managers and others—to protect you from people whose intentions aren't necessarily pure. It's hard to do that for yourself, because it's your *job* to be vulnerable and wide-open as an artist.

## GET A LIFE

The biggest mistake is to make your life all about acting, whether you're working or not. Instead, live a full life. Let the acting come as a by-product of that, because your life informs your work. The more involved you are in noticing and shaping every aspect of your life, the better actor you become. When you start living a full, rich, diverse life in which creativity plays a part, whether it's painting, poetry, cooking, writing, sitting at a zoo and watching animals, or simple observation—the more of a "life artist" you are—the better an artist on stage and in film and television you become. You have more to draw from. You have a larger palette with which to fill your canvas.

What that meant for me, specifically, was that I couldn't wait for someone to give me an acting job to make me happy. I had to *choose* to be happy. The things that made me happy were finding outlets for my creativity, finding ways to create balance in my life—cultivating relationships with people outside of the industry who had interests other than acting and screenwriting and directing. I find the majority of my balance in nature: hiking and walking and running. I also discovered that yoga is a great tool for an actor. Yoga incorporates breath and body and attention, being present, and Beginner's Mind, which is the best tool for me as an actor. You never want to know what the next moment is going to be: you have an idea of how to shape something, but you want to be present for that surprise. Finding the tools to make my life better eventually made me a better artist.

## THE COST OF FAME

I once went out to dinner with Steve Martin and was amazed to discover that he has no private life outside the four walls of his home. His is a totally public life. It's the same with Tom Cruise, Brad Pitt, and Angelina Jolie; there are certain people who don't have privacy in the public arena. I still have a personal life, and privacy, and I'm grateful for it every second. Maybe once *Dallas* hits in the summer of 2012, I won't. But right now, I can still go out to dinner and not be swarmed at the table. There are people who know who I am, but they don't infringe on me, with people picking through my garbage and taking pictures of me from a tree. That level of the voyeurism is not something I would wish on anyone. I've had a good career, but I haven't had to compromise my personal life in order to have it. What a blessing.

Seeing the other side has given me an appreciation for the fact that tremendous fame at an early age is nearly impossible to process. I'm grateful that I've become more successful at this stage in my career than I was earlier. It would have been much harder to be young and successful and then have it all disappear than to feel that I've built my way here. I'm in a really good place now where I've struck a balance between my career and my personal life and I don't undervalue either one.

Actors have a need to be seen and appreciated. That's a necessary part of what drives your pursuit of acting as a career. The Catch-22 is keeping your life together in spite of the fame. You must find a way to balance the attention that comes when you have a career that is in the public eye. Keep in mind that the fame is not important enough to shape how you live your life. I am aware that it is part of the game, but I'm not living my life because of it and I'm not compromising my work because of it. Once you are no longer able to be the observer in life—which is another one of the best tools for an actor, to be able to observe the human condition—and you become the observed instead, you lose your edge and you lose the opportunity to be a voyeur because everybody behaves differently around you.

Be as observant as you can *before* you become famous. Be present and notice things. Notice yourself. When you're feeling a certain way, what are the behaviors? What happens to your physicality when your heart is racing? What happens when you're tired? As an actor you are a student: it's the study of finding those honest expressions of different human behaviors.

## CAREER CRISIS

I became an actor in the beginning to inspire people to become better human beings. It had nothing to do with fame or money; it had to do with illuminating the human condition. But there came a difficult time when, though I had become somewhat successful, I wasn't enjoying acting anymore. I was doing it because it was a job, and everybody was just punching a clock and trying to produce the product. I had lost my own enjoyment of the process, and I lost my faith in why I was doing what I was doing.

I didn't particularly like the roles I was playing, either. A lot of them were very superficial television guest-star types of things, and I was there serving the plot, but I wasn't making a difference in anyone's lives by doing it. I remember calling my mom up and saying, "I'm lost. I don't know what I'm doing or why I'm doing it anymore." And my mother had the presence of mind to say, "Maybe the roles you're playing aren't making the difference you want them to, maybe not yet. But who you are as a human being when you step on that set, how you treat others and how you see life, that's inspirational and that makes a difference. Don't ever forget that the lives you touch while you're in the process of doing a show make a difference."

> **I can't always control the outcome of the product, even if my intention is good, but I can control the process of how that product is made.**

From that moment I took more power back. I found a way to re-engage my dreams. Now I feel that my job isn't who I'm playing, but who I'm being. I can't always control the outcome of the product, even if my intention is good, but I can control the process of how that product is made. That's where I placed my attention, back on the process and on how I treated other people and how I wanted to be treated.

There isn't any greater gift than being human and being on the journey of self-discovery. Part of the artistry of being an actor is knowing yourself. "To thine own self be true." It's this idea that your life is your work and your work is your life and they feed each other. The more available you are to the vulnerability of being human, the better an artist you are, and the more appreciative you are of the frailty of this thing we call life. It's a privilege to be able to illuminate the human condition and to tell the truth about who we are and why we do what we do. It's a gift, and I'm incredibly blessed to be a practitioner of it. ★

For more from Brenda go to
http://www.nowyoutellmebooks.com/actors.

# SAM WATERSTON

## "Make your way with your friends."

A quintessential American actor, Sam Waterston's career has spanned fifty years, and has included major roles in film, television, and on Broadway. Known for movie roles as diverse as Tom in *The Glass Menagerie* and Nick Carraway in *The Great Gatsby,* he was nominated for an Oscar for his portrayal of Sydney in *The Killing Fields.* On stage, he was nominated for both Tony and Drama Desk Awards for his portrayal of Abraham Lincoln in *Abe Lincoln in Illinois,* and won the Drama Desk Award for *Much Ado About Nothing.* He has practiced fictional law for years as Forrest Bedford in the TV series *I'll Fly Away,* and as again as Jack McCoy in *Law & Order.* In 2011, he fulfilled a dream by playing King Lear on stage in New York. Sam's voice is so well known that he does a recurring segment on *The Colbert Report* called "Sam Waterston Says Things You Should Never Believe in a Trustworthy Manner."

# MAKING A LIVING

## RESOLVE, CONFIDENCE, BRAVERY, TALENT

I used to have a little quote by Abraham Lincoln over one of my light switches. It said, "Always bear in mind that your own resolution to succeed is more important than any other."

When I came to New York to start my career as an actor, I was very determined. Some might assume it was confidence; but when I first arrived, I wanted to get a part, any part. I was lucky enough to land some great roles. And it's true that when you get a taste of really juicy parts, it's perfectly natural to want more and more. Looking back, I'm kind of amazed at the gall of assuming I could play lead roles; but I think it came more from a kind of lack of perspective and a kind of monomaniacal desire to express myself through acting than it did from any kind of supreme confidence.

> **The best motivation for me as a young actor was to feel the fire-breathing dragons of shame, disaster, and failure at my back at all times.**

The best motivation for me as a young actor was to feel the fire-breathing dragons of shame, disaster, and failure at my back at all times.

I'll only say, whoever that guy was, I'm glad he was revved at that time.

Part of an actor's desire to do meaty roles has to do with the desire to go deep—where the wild things are, as Maurice Sendak puts it—to get into scary territory in your own emotional life. That part has nothing to do with confidence at all—I don't think anybody can confidently go in there. I think he or she can go *bravely* in there.

On the other hand, confidence is needed, of course; having confidence applies to, "Are you asking me if I can handle the depth and complexity of the part? Yes, I can handle it." The courage part comes in with, "There's some really weird stuff in this play, and it's disturbing to look at the points of contact with my own personality and life, but I'm willing to go there."

One thing I think actors get a perverse pleasure out of doing, and I include myself in this group, is to wonder at the apparent confidence of other actors who you don't think have any right to it. When perfect confidence starts to look like arrogance, it isn't such a desirable thing.

**Part of an actor's desire to do meaty roles has to do with the desire to go deep ...to get into scary territory in your own emotional life.**

The fact is, when the bright lights are on, and the big cameras are there, and you're working with a lot of famous people, you have to have some gall just to not be intimidated by the circumstances. But the actors who are most fascinating are those who can move past that and have the bravery to let us really see their souls.

## WORKING WITH DIRECTORS

I once played an Indian, and for background I did a lot of reading about Indians. One thing that really struck me was that when some of the Plains Indians had a battle, they would take their lances and they would plant them somewhere in the ground on the battlefield. It was their way of declaring that they would be there fighting all day, whatever comers there were.

Likewise, I believe that one thing really good directors have in common is that they place themselves in the field, on the ground, where the play is taking place. Then in thousands of different ways, depending upon their personalities and their skills and their talents and the way they communicate, they defend that territory all day long. Actors will test whether what they're trying is on real ground or not, so a person who's going to be there all day long is crucial. That's where the actor gets his or her permission to do the necessary work and take the necessary chances.

On the other hand, you work with difficult directors with difficulty! There's no single formula, because there are so many different kinds of good directors and so many different kinds of difficult directors. There are also particular circumstances, such as a rush for time, a sudden loss of somebody playing a central part, money problems, all kinds of stresses and strains that also influence the atmosphere in the rehearsal hall. Working with a difficult director is just one of many variables. I've had some really tough times, but they were really peculiar to the personality of that director.

So I don't think there's any really general prescriptions except for the same ones you use in life, such as counting to ten before you give in to anger, looking at the bright side, keeping a positive outlook, and sucking it up. But difficult directors also sometimes produce excellent results, so keep in mind that the quality of the experience, the pleasure (or not) of the rehearsal, and the quality of the result can be completely separate things. You could have a horrible time and still get a great result. You're not finished just because it's rough in the rehearsal hall.

## CAREER LONGEVITY

Satchel Paige said the best thing about this that I ever heard: "Don't look back. Something might be gaining on you." And I really do think "Don't take a breather" is the best prescription. Jobs tend to lead to other jobs, which tend to lead to other jobs. It's sort of like stringing beads. When you get to the end of the string, that's scary. The best you can do is hold on till you start another string.

## CHOOSING ROLES

Some actors might have a grand plan about moving between theater, film, and television; but I've pretty much taken the most interesting thing that came up at the time. Sometimes it was interesting because of the quality, sometimes because it was a lark, and sometimes because of the other people who were doing it; and other times it was interesting because of the money. I've tried not to choose anything solely for money except for when I've really needed it. If it occasionally comes to that point, try not to feel too bad, because everyone has to make a living.

## DIFFERENT PROCESSES DEPENDING ON THE MEDIUM

There are very different processes involved in acting in film and television as opposed to theater. For me, the easiest way to talk about it is when the "put up or shut up" moment comes. In theater there's a long period of rehearsal; and provided you are not terrifying people with being awful in rehearsal, the first "put up or shut up" moment is when the audience comes.

In the movies and in television, it's every couple of hours, and all day long, every day that you're working. When making movies, it can be days or even weeks in between those moments because of the pace at which movies get shot. That means you have to pace yourself kind of in a different way.

Different people cope with it differently. I used to be of the belief that you needed to stay in your character from the first moment that the movie began shooting until the end.

I've never worked with Daniel Day Lewis, but I believe he stays in character as a matter of habit. In the beginning of my career, I did that on a couple of films; but the truth is, I felt kind of stupid doing it. Since then I've come to think that there's a different but equally good way to do this, and I've seen at least two examples of it: Mia Farrow and Meryl Streep. Both of them are supremely talented at being in the moment. They're knitting, or they are playing with the children, or they are doing something that has absolutely nothing to do with the movie—then they're needed on set, and they put down whatever they are doing, and they walk into the movie and are fully and totally committed to *that* reality. They do the movie for however many minutes or hours it takes, and then they walk out of the movie and they pick up their next reality where they left off.

I've come to believe that, if it works for you, staying in the reality of the movie all day long is wonderful; but there is this alternative way that also works if you can train yourself to simply throw the switch.

However, when doing a play, I try and stay in character for the length of the performance. I go to the theater, get into character and get into costume and makeup, and try to stay in that place during the entire play.

It's not always easy. For example, one of the great challenges of playing Laertes in *Hamlet* is that he's got a lot to do and then there are several acts when he's got nothing to do. And then he comes back in a great rage and has a lot to do. It's very hard to figure out how to manage the downtime.

For me, the best way to handle a part like that is to stay in it, in some sort of semidormancy. Because you can't stay revved up. At least I couldn't. Nor could I go off to other amusements. Especially since the things that make him so explosive at the end are a large complex of very, very strong feelings for the people on the stage. I couldn't figure out any other way to come back on the stage and be with these people without staying in their world.

## NEW YORK OR L.A.?

As far away as New York and Los Angeles are from each other, it's important to figure out how to be in both places at once. The business capital of show business is Los Angeles. But New York has a different way of cooking talent, where everybody's in the same pot together: there aren't great big gates and guards and passes that you have to have. The distance between the top dog and the lowliest person in show business, just like the difference between the richest man in town and the poorest, is much smaller in New York. Everybody lives closer to one another; it feels like a much more open town. That's invaluable, and I think that it shows in the work that actors do. There's an awful lot of unremunerated work that is done in New York that is treated with dignity and respect, and deservedly so, because there's so much talent and energy and dedication going into it.

## SECRETS OF THE LONG RUN

Until I did *Law & Order*, I didn't know what it was like to have a steady job. It's an extraordinary rarity in show business.

Doing a series that ran as long as *Law & Order*, or even something with a modestly long run, the thing that makes or breaks the experience is the way that people learn to live with one another. If there are people whom you might not naturally appreciate as performers or as people, you must either find out how to appreciate them or it's going to be a problem. Those wonderful theater stories that are told about guying or about people sabotaging each other's props or having secret conversations onstage, they're really

**The big lesson of the long run is all about mutual accommodations and respect.**

bone-chilling but also kind of fun to think about. However, that's in theater. During months or years of a film or television production, they really are just not possible. Relationships can come apart; the wheels can come off the forward motion. The big lesson of the long run is all about mutual accommodations and respect.

## LUCK

When my son James, who is also an actor, was at Sundance, he had one of those long, friendly conversations that summertime sometimes allows between the aspiring young and the already arrived with Alan Alda: what are you going to do with your life? James said that he thought that he might want to act as a career. Alan Alda made a face, and James said, "What's the matter? You're having fun; my father's having fun," and Alan Alda said, "My advice would be, if you can possibly avoid acting as a career, avoid it." And then he said, "But if you can't avoid it, then I wish you all the luck in the world, and it's a beautiful thing to do—provided you get to do it."

## WHEN TO QUIT

If acting is something you love, there's a lot of hurt in the question of when to give up pursuing it as a profession. It's horrible; I've seen many good actors deal with it; in fact, there was a period of time during which I dealt with it myself. And I honestly don't have any answer to the question of when at all. There's a lot of hurt in that question.

The only way I came through it was that I got a job before I ever reached any conclusion. The awful thing about acting is somebody has to give you a place to do it. You can write a book, and even if nobody publishes it, you can write another book. But if no one gives you an acting job and helps you to recruit an audience, you really can't act.

# MAKING A LIFE

## STAYING SANE

Meryl Streep said a great thing once, that the ideal for an actor is to be semifamous so you have your privacy but there's no part in the business for which you can't be considered.

Fame hasn't intruded on my life to the point of having ever really disturbed it, for which I'm very grateful. Paparazzi giving me no peace in my private life hasn't really ever been a problem. Maybe people who like my work are nice people, and they don't make pests of themselves. But really, having people tell you that they think your work is good, in the middle of a rainy day when you're running down the street in New York, or Chicago, or Podunk, doesn't do any harm to the day. Having people say, "You're great" isn't exactly a problem. At least, not for me.

## MENTORS

The list is long of people I consider mentors, and they taught me everything I know. Some of it I found out for myself by combining things they had to show me or interesting places they gave me to look. I mean, you're not completely a product of those who have influenced you, but it's hard to exaggerate what they do and how often those lessons come back when you need them.

Of the literally thousands of people who have made me who I am, the first two who came to mind are my father and an acting teacher and director named John Berry.

My father introduced me to the theater. It was something that he was always interested in and had dabbled in during his own youth, and he was an extraordinarily civilized and literate man. He planted the idea that there was gold in them thar hills. He obviously enjoyed performing in theater, and he enjoyed watching it. He put me in a play that he directed when I was six years old, and I got to stay up late at night with the big boys. He was the one who instilled in me the confidence to make it through all the down periods. He was steady and confident that it would work out all right in the end.

John Berry was an acting teacher who took a prep school boy and introduced him to Manhattan (even though we were in Paris

## Theater. It's a wonderful thing.

at the time). He introduced me to the pleasure there is in being disagreeable in front of people and in playing the bad guy, in giving voice to your appetite for contention and loudness and struggle, and in duking it out—and then everybody getting up and taking their bows.

Theater. It's a wonderful thing.

## FINAL ADVICE

My final advice is simply this: make your way with your friends so that no matter where you are, they'll be there with you. ★

For more from Sam go to
http://www.nowyoutellmebooks.com/actors.

# KENT PAUL

## "Make Your Own Path"

K ent Paul's career as a highly respected theater director has so far spanned thirty years. Based in New York City, where he does most of his work, he has directed productions in locales as far-flung as Florida, Massachusetts, North Carolina, and Iceland.

After graduation from Harvard College, Paul trained as an actor at The Neighborhood Playhouse in New York City. When work as an actor was hard to find, he accepted work as a producer and publicist at the Cincinnati Playhouse, where "part of my job was to drive actors to press interviews. Sometimes the interviews were in Dayton, which was thirty miles away. Actors in rehearsal are always scared. On the ride, they'd say, 'I can't make this work,' or 'I don't know how to say this.' I was forever saying, 'Well, maybe it's about this,' or 'Why don't you try this?' They'd suggest I try directing, and I'd say, 'No, I'm too shy; I have no visual imagination.'"

But the opportunity arose, and he directed his first full play at the Cincinnati Playhouse. That was it. "After directing one play, I was obsessed. I don't feel quite so dramatic these days, but I used to say my life didn't begin until I started directing."

Paul has worked with three generations of theater actors. Over the years, he has noticed common threads among those actors who have made successful careers and successful lives, and those who have not. Here is some of what he's found.

# MAKING A LIVING

## AUDITIONS

Let's start with auditions.

When an actor walks into an audition, what I'm looking for is naturalness. Curiosity. Vitality. Openness. Skill with language. Training is important, and, in some measure, experience. I suppose attractiveness is an aspect of vitality, although by attractiveness I don't necessarily mean conventional beauty. When I find an actor with whom I want to work, it's always because I saw his or her ability to come alive in imaginary circumstances, a release of secrets and fantasy.

When preparing for an audition, it's a good idea to dress for the part; hair is an aspect of that. I often tell young actors to dress better for auditions. They tend to dress down—to look as though they're working class because somehow that means they're serious—whereas often the play I'm casting (right now it's one by Shaw) is a play of language, with characters who are educated or stylish, people who have self-conscious identities.

Keep in mind that nervousness is natural. By far the best way to deal with nerves is to take to heart Sanford Meisner's dictate: "What you do doesn't depend upon you; it depends upon what the other person does." Get the attention off yourself. If you're reading, then the attention goes to the person who's reading with you. If you're doing a monologue, your attention goes to the people who are listening. That way you can't know exactly what you're going to do with the lines. But you should be as familiar with them as possible. Memorize the scene, but still hold the book. You should hold the book for

**WHAT KENT PAUL IS LOOKING FOR IN AUDITIONS**

- Naturalness
- Curiosity
- Vitality
- Openness
- Skill with language
- Training
- Experience
- Attractiveness (not necessarily conventional beauty)
- Knowing your lines but holding your book

For more go to http://www.nowyoutellmebooks.com/actors

two reasons: No matter how experienced you are, if you've just learned the material, sometimes you forget. Also, once you get rid of the book, it invites a different level of expectation.

Once actors are cast, the qualities that make me want to work with them again are emotional resourcefulness and openness to collaboration with the director, even if I'm asking them to go against a first impulse. Years ago, I directed the former star of a television series in *The Glass Menagerie* in North Carolina. The audience was seated on three sides, with the fewest number of people sitting in what would be the front of the stage in a proscenium. But the woman was used to playing on a proscenium and had no experience with a thrust stage. So I would say, "When you're saying that, would you mind walking over to that chair and slowly turning it around and eventually sitting down in it?" Of course that would mean she'd turn her back to the center section, and she'd say, "No, I don't want to do that."

"Couldn't we just try it?"

She'd say, "Well, I know that if I try it, you'll say you like it and then I'll have to keep it."

And I said, "Yes, that's probably the way it will go."

Eventually it got staged.

To the list of why I'd work with someone over and over, I'd add skill with language.

> I love to hear language dance in the theater.

I love to hear language dance in the theater. But in a natural way.

I'm sometimes asked if it matters to me on a basic level whether an actor is difficult or causes me a lot of grief. You know what? I don't care *what* happens in rehearsal as long as the play turns out well. I don't care what difficulties I am presented with, what grief. I love working with the same actors over and over. In fact, when possible, I make it happen. As long as the performance works, I'm pretty forgiving. Lynn Redgrave was demanding. And my friend Sam Waterston asks a lot of questions in rehearsal. But I miss Lynn, and I would do another play with Sam tomorrow.

It used to be a hallmark of stars that they were difficult. For example, Kathleen Nolan came into the theater as Wendy to Mary Martin's *Peter Pan*. To this day, Kathleen wears white the first day of rehearsal because Mary Martin told her that the star should wear white the first day. It used to be in the theater that the people who played leading roles, the "stars," could be quite difficult and that would be tolerated. But people's careers stop now because they're difficult, however good they are. So young actors need to figure out how to get along with the director, and how to get along with their fellow actors, or their careers won't happen.

## Exceptional people get to make their own rules.

At the same time, exceptional people get to make their own rules. Sam always had a sense of himself as a star. But he started out as a star. He replaced Austin Pendleton, his classmate at Yale, in Arthur Kopit's *Oh Dad, Poor Dad*. I remember early on when he was staying with me for a bit, him being on the phone with Robert Brustein, who was begging him to come to Yale to do plays, and Sam said, "No, no, I'm working on my New York career." He made his own rules from the start.

But memories are long. [Director] Sydney Pollack told me a story about when he made the film *Absence of Malice* with Paul Newman. One day Sydney said to Paul, "My friend Mark Rydell has tried to get you in picture after picture. You always turn him down."

And Paul Newman said, "When Mark Rydell was at The Neighborhood Playhouse, he dated Joanne's [Woodword] roommate, and he didn't treat her very well." So he never wanted to work with him. People do remember how you act.

## WHO MAKES IT AND WHO DOESN'T

Besides luck, there are two differences between a talented actor who makes it and one who doesn't. They are stamina and resourcefulness.

Stamina means you keep going even when no one is giving you a job and you wonder whether you're in the right field. You're obsessed. You can't stop marching.

Because the truth is, if you can stop marching, you should.

I've known Broadway actor Boyd Gaines since he was a student at Juilliard. He's since won four Tony Awards. When Boyd was in the Broadway production of *Journey's End*, he took some people I had brought for that evening for a tour of the old Belasco Theater, which was about to be redone. Afterward, he and I were standing outside, and two young women who had attached themselves to the group said, "Mr. Gaines, we're students at NYU. Do you have any advice for people just getting into the theater?"

Boyd answered, "If you can possibly do something else, do. If you have to do it, know that it's a lot of agony for a few exquisite moments. But those moments are exquisite."

That's what I mean by stop marching if you can. Boyd told the truth. Making a living as an actor *is* going to bring you a lot of agony. No sane person should put up with it if he or she can make another choice.

When people ask me, "How do I get started as a director?" my response is, "If you have to ask me that question, you're already lost."

The whole thing about being an artist is that you make your own path. You don't ask permission.

Recently an artist named Louise Bourgeois had a big show at the Guggenheim. It made such an impression on me that I went twice and later went to see a documentary about her. This lovely woman was in her mid-nineties, and she was very matter-of-fact. She said, "I make art because it makes me feel better. It makes me happy."

She and her father had a somewhat embattled relationship; she was an artist and that was work in which he never had taken any interest. Still, her father's death just flattened her. She took to her bed for months. Then one day she got up and went back into the studio.

That's stamina; after a hard blow, getting out of bed and back to work.

The other thing that someone needs for a career besides stamina is resourcefulness. You just keep looking. It means making opportunities for yourself. It means doing anything and everything to keep working.

I once was doing Arthur Miller's *A Memory of Two Mondays* to be followed by three of O'Neill's "Sea Plays." So I was rehearsing *Mondays*; and with virtually the same cast, I was set to do the Sea Plays. An actor came in and did a wonderful audition, but I said, "I have a little company, and I've worked out who will play in *A Memory of Two Mondays* and move into the O'Neill plays. I'm sorry, but I can't fit you into the scheme I've worked out."

And in a very friendly but clear way, he said to me, "You mean after the audition I just did, you're not going to cast me?"

I said, "Uh, let me think about it." And you know what? I figured out a different scheme and worked him into the company, and of course he was just superb. So, resourcefulness means staying alert to all the opportunities. But when you're really right for something and the audition doesn't go well, it also means calling the director, or calling the casting director, and saying, "I was just awful. Can I read again?" It's breaking the rules. It's doing everything that people tell you not to do.

> **[Success means] breaking the rules. It's doing everything that people tell you not to do.**

I also suggest reaching out to directors and playwrights whose work you particularly like. If you see a play by a new playwright that you think is quite remarkable, somehow find a way to get word to the playwright that you like his or her work and would be interested in being considered for that playwright's next play. And the same thing with directors.

As a director, I do the same thing. Last fall I saw a play off-Broadway, at the Vineyard, that had gotten a very poor review in the *New York Times*. But I thought it was just magical. So I wrote to the playwright.

Also consider getting in touch with theaters that are doing the kind of material you'd like to be doing. It's probably a good idea to write to the artistic director and say "The next time you're in New York, could I audition for you?" or, "I'd be willing to come to Hartford to show you my monologues."

It's also important to cherish and stay in contact with the people you come into the theater with and whom you really like. So much has to do with luck and with personal contacts. Keep in touch with people you trust and admire. Combine forces with them whenever possible.

> **Keep in touch with people you trust and admire. Combine forces with them whenever possible.**

# MAKING A LIFE

## THE HABITS OF A SUCCESSFUL ACTOR

What are the most important habits of the successful actor? Resilience and adaptability. No question.

Resilience means that you don't take personally not being cast. It means that you realize, even when you get a bad review, that the reviewer may be an idiot or not but that still your name has appeared unfavorably in public—but you have to keep working.

Adaptability means being ready to do a Fringe play for a hundred dollars after making your Broadway debut. Adaptability means being able to do Molière as well as Sam Shepard. A willingness to go to Minneapolis if that's where you get to play Hamlet.

> **Adaptability means being able to do Molière as well as Sam Shepard.**

When I think of actors who have made good lives for themselves as well as a good living, certainly some measure of self-respect is key. Healthy friendships or relationships are sustaining. It's also helpful to find other things in life that bring you great joy so that if you're very depressed about a job you didn't get and you can find a concert to go to that will leave you joyous, that will help. ★

For more from Kent go to
http://www.nowyoutellmebooks.com/actors.

# PHOTO CREDITS

**Lynn Redgrave Photos**
As Helena in *A Midsummer Night's Dream*, 1961
Photo by Sandra Lousada

Lynn, Vanessa, and Jemma Redgrave in *Three Sisters*, 1991
Photo by John Haynes

*Shakespeare for My Father*, 1993
Photo by Joan Marcus

With Ruth Gordon in *Mrs. Warren's Profession*, 1976
Photo by Sy Friedman

**David Oyelowo Photos**
Eric Williams/ DR Photo

Eric Williams/ DR Photo

Headshot courtesy of David Oyelowo

With his wife, Jessica, at the opening of *Rise of the Planet of the Apes*
Courtesy of Shutterstock

**Pauley Perrette Photos**
©Janet Mayer

Photo by Adam Bouska
Courtesy of www.noh8campaign.com

Headshot courtesy of Pauley Perrette

©Janet Mayer

## Michael O'Neill Photos
With his wife and daughters
Courtesy of Michael O'Neill

Headshot courtesy of Michael O'Neill

From *Grey's Anatomy*
Courtesy of ABC

## Charles Busch Photos
With Julie Halston
Photo by David Rodgers

Charles Busch
Photo by David Rodgers

Headshot courtesy of Charles Busch

Young Charles
Courtesy of Charles Busch

## Julia Motyka Photos
Julia, age 4
Courtesy of Julia Motyka

As Ariel in *The Tempest*
Photo by Alexander Weisman
Courtesy of Pioneer Theater Company

As Rachel in *Reckless*
Courtesy of Julia Motyka

As Lena Lingard in *My Àntonia*
Courtesy of Julia Motyka

## Brian Stokes Mitchell Photos
As Don Quixote in *Man of La Mancha*
Photo by Joan Marcus

Photo by Beth Kelly

Photo by Beth Kelly

With his mom
Courtesy of Brian Stokes Mitchell

## Eden Sher Photos
Courtesy of Shutterstock

Courtesy of Shutterstock

Courtesy of Eden Sher

## Michael McKean Photos
As Gloucester with Sam Waterston in *King Lear*
Photo by Joan Marcus

©Janet Mayer

With his dad, Gil McKean
Courtesy of Michael McKean

As Arthur in *Superior Donuts*
Photo by Robert J. Saferstein

## Alexandra Neil Photos
With her mother, Edith Thompson, at Gay Head, Martha's Vineyard
Courtesy of Alexandra Neil

With Andrew McCarthy in *Marathon of One-Act-Plays,* 1985
Photo by Valerie Brea Ross

As Candida in Tom Stoppard's *Rock 'n' Roll*, 2008
Courtesy of Alexandra Neil

As Mrs. Ellis in *NoNAMES*
Courtesy of Alexandra Neil

## Joseph Kolinski Photos
As Lysander in *A Midsummer Night's Dream*
Courtesy of Joseph Kolinski

Thomas M. Suda, S. Epatha Merkerson and Joe
Singing "Friendship"
Courtesy of Joseph Kolinski

With Anne Kavanagh in *Six Dance Lessons in Six Weeks*
Photo by Reinhard Reidinger
Courtesy of Vienna's English Theater

With Lynne Wintersteller in *Meet Me in St. Louis*
Photo by Bruce Bennett
Courtesy of Theater Under the Stars

## Brenda Strong Photos
With her son Zakery Henri
Courtesy of Shutterstock

Headshot courtesy of Brenda Strong

©Janet Mayer

With the cast of *Desperate Housewives*
Courtesy of Shutterstock

## Sam Waterston Photos
©Janet Mayer

Courtesy of Sam Waterston

©Janet Mayer

As King Lear
Photo by Joan Marcus

# ABOUT THE AUTHORS

**SHERIDAN SCOTT,** the primary coauthor of the *Now You Tell Me!* series, has edited half a dozen *Chicken Soup for the Soul* books as well as serving as a coauthor. An award winning biographer, she has been a staff writer for five national magazines and has ghostwritten for dozens of celebrities, as well as hundreds of regular folks.

**CHRIS WILLMAN** is one of the top celebrity journalists in Los Angeles. He writes for *TV Guide, New York Magazine, Entertainment Weekly, Yahoo! Music, Rolling Stone,* and other publications. He is the author of the book *Rednecks and Bluenecks: The Politics of Country Music.*

**TODD COLEMAN** is a Los Angeles-based journalist, filmmaker, and media consultant. He has interviewed almost seventeen hundred Hollywood leaders as an entertainment and media journalist. A graduate of NYU film school, he currently has two books, a feature screenplay, and various web-based projects in development.

A portion of the proceeds fom this book will go
to support The Actors Fund
www.actorsfund.org

**Would you like a mentor? If so visit www.nowyoutellmebooks.com/actors and join the conversation.**